€ 0.3?

(German)

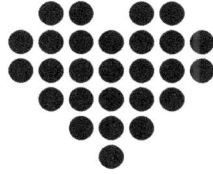

LOVE
Art, Ideas, Music, Politics

The Love Collective

Kembla Books
Wollongong

Love: Art, Ideas, Music, Politics
ISBN 978-0-6488258-0-7

First hardback edition June 2020

Book design by Justin Westgate, Antipode Studio

Kembla Books
Wollongong, NSW, Australia
kemblabooks.com

A catalogue record for this
work is available from the
National Library of Australia

Acknowledgement

The Love Collective acknowledges the Traditional Custodians of the land. Our meetings and festivals have occurred on the lands of the Dharawal and Yuin people, which have never been ceded. As we share our knowledge, we seek to learn from the knowledge embedded within the Aboriginal custodianship of Country and pay thanks for the love of Country performed by the Dharawal and Yuin peoples. The 2014 *Love: Arts, Ideas, Music, Politics* festival took place in the Sydney suburb of Minto which is on Dharawal land. Here we were welcomed to Country by Uncle Ivan, who outlined the continuing significance of the land on which we met. The 2017 festival took place in Wollongong on Djeera/Mount Keira, which is a culturally and historically significant site. Here we were welcomed to Country by Wadi Wadi man Mark Patruski. The Mountain and the Five Islands off the Wollongong coast are integral to the dreaming of local Aboriginal peoples. The Mountain's summit has been used for ceremonies and includes a significant women's business site. These places have been shaped by millennia of Aboriginal care and we seek to listen to and learn from Aboriginal understandings of love, healing, respect, responsibility, and reciprocity.

Welcome to Country 2014 by Uncle Ivan.
Photo by Ella Pusell.

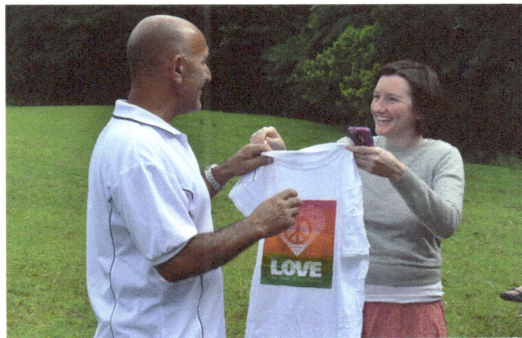

Welcome to Country 2017 by Mark Paturski with MC Melanie Barnes.
Photo by Nina Kourea.

Love 2017 camp site at Djeera/Mount Keira.
Photo by Ella Pusell.

CONTENTS

Introduction
The Love Collective

Cali Pusell welcomes participants to *Love 2017*.
Photo by Ella Pusell.

Love: Art, Ideas, Music, Politics began in Wollongong in 2013, when a group of people started a reading group about love. For most of us this was the latest action in a long series of reading groups, activist projects, cultural activities and academic endeavours all based loosely in Wollongong on the south coast of New South Wales. We were particularly influenced by the upsurge in the worldwide feminist movement and the global campaign for equal love. When the University of Wollongong decided to axe its Gender Studies major course in 2012 on the grounds that it was not 'cost effective', a group of students and staff at the university organised a Feminist Society (FemSoc) free school, where lectures and discussions on feminism and the struggle for gender equality could take place outside the classroom. Many of those who joined the love reading group had participated in FemSoc, and its ethic of autonomous self-education and democratic discussion informed the operation of the group.

A number of grassroots initiatives were happening in Wollongong that year. Besides FemSoc, there was a significant campaign against coal seam gas mining, the launch of the Illawarra Aboriginal Solidarity Group, and a growing urban permaculture movement. What seemed to be lacking, however, was a sense of how such movements related to one another. Much of this activity appeared fractured and there was a palpable sense of alienation and loneliness felt by many within these separate movements. Some of those who became involved in the love reading group had also been active in left-wing and progressive organisations for many years. There was a common perception that these groups often ignored or neglected interpersonal relations and more caring ways of collectively organising. Over time, it became apparent that what was missing was an appreciation of the politics of love.

The politics of love

Fittingly enough, the first major text the love reading group tackled was *All About Love: New Visions* by the black feminist writer bell hooks. hooks' work uses her personal experience as a black woman growing up in America and her experiences of gendered and racial oppression in her academic work as material for discussing the lack of love in a society dominated by sexist, patriarchal, white supremacist capitalism. She explores the possibilities inherent in love as a practice of freedom for confronting and overcoming these intersecting forms of oppression. Importantly, hooks doesn't simply posit love as an ideal to which we should aspire, but locates it within existing relationships and practices. She alerts us to the existence of love in our lives, even when it is complicated by hierarchies of gender, race and class. Her work and her deeply personal engagement with the struggle for more love had a major impact on all of us and led to wide-ranging discussions about our personal and political experiences of love and loss.

The love reading group was largely made up of people who already knew each other but it helped create a new collective and a sense of common purpose that eventually coalesced into a plan to organise a festival, where the ideas we were discussing in the reading group could be put into practice. As the group continued to meet throughout 2013, we decided to issue a callout for 'A Planning Meeting to Organise a Festival of Love'. We aimed at a fully embodied exploration of love in action, proposing in the original call-out for the event that:

> The festival might be thought of as a temporary 'commune' based on a love ethic in which everybody is encouraged to look out for one another, pitch in with food preparation, childcare, cleaning and helping ensure everything runs smoothly.

Part of the vision of the love festival was to remind ourselves that we are not alone and that there are other people like us who are struggling for social change and trying to develop more caring, democratic and equal social relations in a multitude of ways. The festival was conceived as a project of commoning – of drawing together the various individuated experiences of social solidarity and creating a temporary space in which we could find one another. By inviting contributors to come to love through art, ideas, music or politics we hoped to create the widest possible scope for people to connect with the central idea of the event. Our aim was to recognise and to celebrate the existing forms of love in these overlapping networks and solidarity teams and to facilitate the further interweaving of these networks as an act of love expanding love.

The love festival

As we started to tell people about the festival we were struck by how often we were met with uncomfortable smirks and sniggers. Some of these reactions seemed to be prompted by the idea that the love festival must be a kind of orgy. This image seems to be tied to our stereotypical understandings of the counter-culture of the 1960s and 1970s, when 'sex, drugs and rock 'n' roll' were said to form the basis of student and peace movements. However, the discomfort people experience when talking about the love festival also

Love 2014 poster.
Design by Justin Westgate.

had a deeper meaning. It was symptomatic of the more general discomfort that many of us feel when we try to talk about love. In the modern era, love has become a largely private experience and been confined within the romantic couple and the family. We called our festival *Love: Art, Ideas, Music, Politics* because we wanted to make explicit the link between love and all of these diverse social practices. We wanted to re-inject politics with love and love with politics by creating a space where people could come together to talk about love in a serious way.

Putting the idea of a love festival into practice took nearly a year of planning and the first festival took place in April 2014. It was held at Minto Bush Camp, a property in western Sydney that once served as a retreat for the Communist Party of Australia. The event attracted about 70 people over two days, many of whom stayed overnight in cabins and tents. The festival

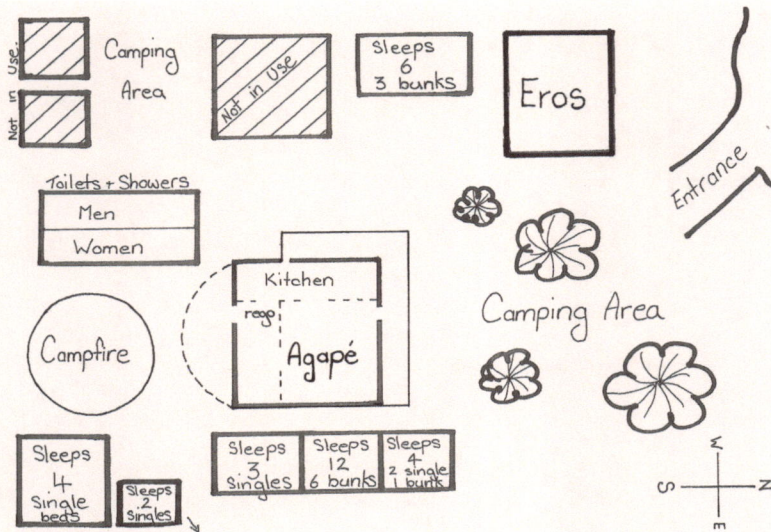

Love 2014 Site Map.
Drawing by Sharon Pusell.

Love 2017 Site Map.
Drawing by Sharon Pusell.

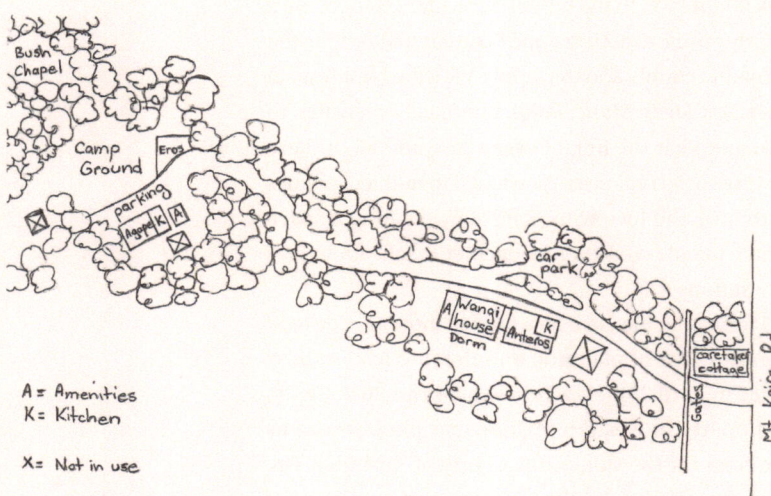

festival we decided to organise a more ambitious three-day schedule and to hold a lantern parade, for which we prepared with separate open workshops in the lead-up to the festival. We also gave more attention to encouraging the involvement of children with a variety of children's activities, kid's spaces, a pop-up circus playground and facilitated children's discussion about love. Our increased experience and grander ambitions for the second festival were repaid when more than one hundred people took part over the course of the event.

'By inviting contributors to come to love through art, ideas, music or politics we hoped to create the widest possible scope for people to connect with the central idea of the event.'

The formal event program was again based mainly on workshops in which we asked facilitators to maximise the participation of all of the attendees. We issued an open-call for workshop presenters through our networks but we also directly invited many individuals whom we thought might connect the festival with their solidarity teams and communities and thereby facilitate wider participation. The workshop subjects were diverse and we encouraged workshops based on discussion or on other forms of creative practices. At the 2017 love festival, for example, creative workshops included explorations of love through singing, creative writing and dance. Discussion-based workshops looked at topics such as compassion, protecting oneself from abuse, love, sex and democracy, death, the politics of love, men in love, permaculture and love of the earth and the question 'What is love?' An important part of the formal program was the provision for all-in sessions at the beginning and end of the festival so that potential strangers could get to know one another better to further facilitate participation in the workshops and informal social interaction.

As part of the vision of a 'temporary commune' we wanted as much as possible to encourage people to join us for the whole festival weekend. Today, our time is increasingly splintered across multiple relationships, jobs, media and projects and we felt that in order to make time for love we needed to create the potential for uninterrupted time together in a peaceful environment. We therefore organised a food team responsible for catering and tried to create a program that balanced workshops and formal sessions with ample time and space for people to do the informal work of love by hanging out together, talking and attending to one another's needs. We organised night time concerts at both events as well as a selection of films that related

program included a range of workshops facilitated by those interested in different aspects of love, as well as film screenings, and a party with DJs playing music on the Saturday night. There was also plenty of time for discussions and self-organised activities around the formal program. At the conclusion of the festival we held an all-in session to discuss the question 'What is Love?' in order to let people have a final say about what they thought of the festival. The common response from participants was that they loved the festival and were keen to attend similar events in the future.

The positive feedback we received about the event motivated the organising collective to reconvene in 2016 to begin preparations for a second love festival. The second event, held in 2017, was similar to the first, but this time we held it closer to home at the Kum-ba-yah Camp, a Girl Guides camp nestled in the foothills of Djeera/Mt Keira in Wollongong. At this to different struggles around love. The second festival also featured a virtual reality experience, artistic and interactive displays. We were pleasantly surprised by how successfully our 'temporary commune' functioned. There was no shortage of volunteers to help with the food preparation, childcare and cleaning.

The Love festivals were not-for-profit events and we aimed to make them as affordable as possible. All labour was voluntary and we received a range of financial, supply and resource gifts which meant the price was determined by the cost of the site hire and food. At the 2017 festival, full price for the weekend was $65, with a concession/student/part-time wage price of $45, and day visitor price of $20. These prices included all meals, drinks, activities and accommodation. As we explained on the festival website, if people were unable to afford these prices we understood, and they could still attend without payment. Participants were able to bring a tent and camp on site or stay in a dormitory. As there were a limited number of beds, priority was given to anyone who might find it difficult to camp. The collective also offered transport from the nearest train station to the festival sites.

New horizons

Both festivals revolved around the creation of affective spaces which were open to diversity and common activity and where people could think about love, talk about love, learn more about loving and experience more profound connections with each other and the earth that sustains us. Those in attendance warmly embraced a festival wide commitment to creating joyful, celebratory and loving activities, events and spaces for connection and affinity while respecting and accommodating differences, where there was no attempt to promote love by enforcing forms of identity, unity, or conformity.

In the final all-in sessions at both festivals, participants talked about their experiences. For many, the festivals helped them to rethink and reintegrate experiences of activist burnout and reconnect their political ideals with their desires for love, fun and community. At these concluding sessions people expressed a common desire to keep the festival going rather than going home, and most attendees were keen to have another festival as soon as possible. However, after organising two large-scale events we wanted a change of pace and to take a different approach to furthering our love politics. The idea for this book was born out of this desire to keep nurturing the network of solidarity teams that have developed out of the festival in a different form.

Top: 'Camp Fun'.
Drawing by Matt Kocher.

Above: Writing with Love
Workshop at *Love 2017*.
Photo by Nina Kourea.

During the love festivals people were able to come closer together and to get to know each other better. They were able to share resources, knowledges, ways of doing things, cultural forms and experiences, enriching those in attendance and the communities they returned to while opening up new horizons for creativity, deepening exchanges and fostering solidarity. We are confident that these experiences of love in practice have resonated throughout people's lives and have demonstrated and nurtured communities of struggle by building the capacity to love through cooperation and collaboration to produce more love.

> *'...these experiences of love in practice have resonated throughout people's lives.'*

A challenge that often presents itself in the work of the love collective is how we can actively incorporate our ideas about love and the world we want to build into our day-to-day lives. We try to bring the ideas discussed at the love festivals into our organising by practicing love as an everyday act of resistance. We do this by focusing on building strong, supportive and caring relationships, both within the love collective and with other people. Because of this, the love collective has not remained the same across the span of years it has existed but has welcomed people of different ages, experiences and perspectives into its fold. In this sense the collective is a dynamic entity that provides a space for us to learn from one another, grow together and build strong interpersonal relationships that foster thriving communities. Over the course of organising two love festivals in 2014 and 2017 we assembled a group of committed organisers, a broad network of enthusiastic participants and supporters and a body of knowledge and experience about love and its practice. We drew on our existing networks and solidarity teams and invited them to join in loving conversations with one another. By doing so, we helped to strengthen the bonds between the multitude of smaller loving communities that make up Wollongong and beyond.

Love book

In 2018, the love collective distributed a call for contributions to this book saying:

> In order to continue the love project we would like to compile a book that draws on the ideas and experiences of the love festivals. We are looking for essays, fiction, poetry, artworks, songs, reflections, reviews, images, recipes, photographs, designs or other contributions to the volume. We would particularly encourage contributions from participants and workshop organisers from either of the two festivals but are open to pitches from anyone for whom the notion of love evokes a creative

response. We have a broad understanding of love and are interested in contributions that celebrate the power of love or explore its meaning. Creative contributions that explore love through movement, art or sound (provided they can be reproduced in some way on the printed page) are particularly welcome. Contributions should address the central theme of love and be broadly in keeping with the ethos of the festival.

Most of those who responded to the call-out had been involved in the love festivals, some were members of the organising collective, some had attended the love reading groups, some had facilitated workshops, and others had only just heard of the love group and/or the festivals via the call for contributions to the book.

The contributions to this book form an eclectic range of responses to the idea of *Love: Art, Ideas, Music, Politics*. Nick Southall, Annette Maguire, Sunil Menon, John Rainford, Kristy Newton, Bridget Dougherty, Justin Westgate, Mark Gawne and Alexander Brown provided longer essays reflecting on different aspects of love. These longer contributions are interleaved with a variety of creative and reflective pieces. These include poems by Milena Cifali and John Passant, a song by Paul Spencer, a reflection on the Heart Song workshops held at the two festivals by workshop coordinator Perla Aura, and a piece of creative nonfiction by Sheryl Wiffen. Jackie Bailey and Jodi Phillis both contributed essays on love during the process of death and dying. There are also two interviews with workshop organisers. Alexander Brown interviewed Gavin Moores and Nick Southall interviewed Alice and Ruth Kocher. Sharon Pusell evokes the colourful lantern parade from the second festival with instructions for making a heart lantern. Shining Rainbow shares her artwork, exhibited at the 2014 event and Alison Jones reflects on the nature of porridge, the delicious breakfast cereal she served with love at both love festivals. We are grateful to Nina Kourea, Cali Pusell and Ella Pusell for the photographs which illustrate this book, which convey the atmosphere at the two events. Drawings were contributed by Matt Kocher, Siobhan Christian and Jodi Phyllis. Justin Westgate designed our festival posters and this book.

We are pleased that so many participants and interested people have sent us the contributions you will find in the following pages. The love festivals have been important events in all of our lives and our ongoing work on this project continues to give our lives meaning as we integrate the knowledge, experience and relationships generated at the festivals into our lives and struggles. We hope you enjoy this book.

Love 2017 poster.
Design by Justin Westgate.

Come with Love
Milena Cifali

Some like it hard some like it soft some like it
   sunny side up
Some like it scrambled some like it poached
Some like it with a slice of toast
Some like it with a bit of crumpet
Some like to blow their own trumpet
Some like it low some might get high
Some on the ground some in the sky
Some like it curly some like it straight
Some love to agitate
Some like to hashtag some like to gasbag
Some on diets while some are starving
Some are crying some are laughing
Some like it wet some like it dry
Some let life pass them by
Some like the motion some like commotion
Some disenchanted
Some disenfranchised
Some teach history some seek mystery
Some like to tease
Some hard to please
Some half empty some half full
Some like to push and some to pull
Some are needy some are greedy
Some feel guilty
Some are forgiven
Some are lazy some are driven
Some like it big some like it small
Some don't like it at all
Some full of passion
Some slaves to fashion
Some pessimistic
Some altruistic
Some become great some disappear
Some filled with peace some filled with fear
Some speak the truth some like to shout
Some with a conscience some without
Some come too early some too late
Some come with love some come with hate
Don't come with hate come with love
I repeat all the above.

The Awesome (feat. John Passant)
performing at *Love 2017*.
Photo by Ella Pusell.

What is Love?

Nick Southall

Love is what makes you smile when you're tired.
  – Terri, aged 4

Love is what's in the room with you at Christmas if you stop opening presents and listen.
  – Bobby, aged 7

You really shouldn't say 'I love you' unless you mean it. But if you mean it, you should say it a lot. People forget.
  – Jessica, aged 8

What is Love? Is it a feeling, an instinct, an emotion, an ideology, a passion, a project, an activity, a form of power, struggle, work, wealth, action, a need, desire, intention, dream, illusion, utopia, or is it all of these, and more? To conclude the *Love: Art, Ideas, Music, Politics* festival held in 2014 those in attendance discussed the question posed above, sharing a diversity of views, experiences, and understandings of love. In the lead-up to *Love: Art, Ideas, Music, Politics 2017* there was an opportunity to revisit this question. So, I wrote this piece in preparation for a festival workshop on the question – What is Love?

'Love is more easily experienced than defined.'

I've previously written about love and Christmas, love and advertising, love and revolution, about love as a movement, and a form of defence against hate, violence and terror. Yet I continue to struggle with the question of what love is. Love is complex because it's socially, economically, politically and culturally constructed. How we imagine love – what we think it is and how we think about it – is learned during childhood and developed through our relationships with each other and the world around us. What it's like to love and be loved depends on social and individual histories and our understandings and beliefs about love change as we change, as those around us change, and as society changes. In a previous article, I pointed out that most books on the subject of love work hard to avoid giving clear definitions. According to Morgan Scott Peck love lacks clarity because it 'is too large, too deep ever to be truly understood or measured or limited within the framework of words' and 'our use of the word 'love' is so generalised and unspecific as to severely interfere with our understanding of love.' None-the-less, when asked to produce a short response, I usually define love as the struggle to create, maintain and develop caring social relations.

John Armstrong's philosophical work, *Conditions of Love*, explores 'the task of separating the many themes, the many strands of thought that, are entangled around our word 'love'.' He argues that love isn't a single thing but a complex of different concerns which suggests some of the problems of love. 'When we try to love we are not actually trying to undertake a single endeavour; rather, we are trying to do a whole range of different, and sometimes not very compatible, things simultaneously.'

All the feels

People often think of love as an emotional reaction, as a 'force or power inside the body', which spontaneously

Above: What is Love? workshop at *Love 2017*. Photo by Nina Kourea.

erupts out of us. Love can produce a range of bodily processes and sensations, chemical reactions, and feelings which we may not clearly perceive, understand, or appear to have control over. But how we interpret and react to our bodies and emotions again reflects our personal and collective circumstances, histories, cultures, and ideologies.

There are various and contested definitions and understandings of emotions, what they are, how they're created and how they're experienced. Radical theorists explore emotions as structures of feeling that give meaning to relational experience, arguing you cannot understand love as an emotion from a consideration of the individual, because love is socially constructed, shaped by acculturation and inter-personal relations. Also, rather than being distinct, emotion and rational thinking can be seen as different ways of regarding the same process. Human interaction involves affecting others, being affected by others and acting on those affects, which then affects others, and so on. These social interactions are power relations and emotions/ thought play a crucial role in them. Emotions are thus states of consciousness that go beyond sensations, feelings, expressions, or moods. They involve the recognition, combination, and alteration of these things.

Many theorists have written about the importance of 'emotion work' – trying to change in degree or quality an emotion or feeling, in order to manage them – and how this can be done. Deborah Lupton explains how discourses on emotions, including 'feeling rules' (shared norms that influence how people try to feel), help to shape and reshape our emotions as continuous projects of subjectivity. Different cultures construct different rules and various prescriptions about what we're supposed to feel about love and there's a constant struggle around these 'feeling rules' as they are contested, rise and fall, ebb and flow. These emotion struggles occur both within society and our own consciousness. Therefore, rapid individual or social change can bring about a lack of clarity about what the 'rules' of love are, whether there are any rules, and if they should be obeyed. As with the attempt to define love, the emotions of love are uncertain, and we often encounter situations where we can't put our feelings into words, or find it hard to identify which emotion(s) we're experiencing.

The power of love

Love is the result of our action, our caring activities. Since all relationships are power relations, love is about who has power, who has power over us, whether we have power to do what we want, and whether power is shared. I've written elsewhere about some of the limits capitalism places on love and it's helpful to appreciate how the dominant social system restricts what we can be, as well as appreciating how much power we have to overcome these limits.

In an article about love and what it could be, Natasha Lennard explored some of the problems with how we tend to perceive 'romantic love' and how 'the mystification of romantic love has been particularly damaging to women.' Renata Grossi explains that romantic love is often seen by feminist/queer theory as oppressive, patriarchal and heteronormative, while others see love as a site of resistance, transformation and agency, embodying 'a radical and permissive ideology.' Many, like bell hooks, seek to salvage and elevate love as a radical and healing practice, arguing for a definition of love as a mutual, life-affirming choice and practice – a verb as well as a noun.

For Natasha Lennard 'the key questions are not about what love *is* but about what love *does*. Or perhaps more precisely, what we can do with it.' Pessimistic views of love suppose that it weakens, disarms or enslaves us, making us needy, or dependent. Love is often seen as outside of our control, inevitable and overpowering. Many definitions of love 'emphasise its spontaneity' and 'refuse to acknowledge that it could involve any element of effort or intention.' Here the separation between love and our labour is both misguided and conservative, 'to the extent that it suggests that we have no agency, no power to shape the world as we recreate it.'

'It is one thing to feel loving towards someone, another to translate this feeling into words and actions which make the other person feel loved.' – John Armstrong

Love is a practical matter – it involves caring for people. If love involves a desire 'to do what is good for others' – we require an understanding of what that 'good' is. Often love is considered to be about caring for others like you care for yourself. But what if you don't care for yourself, or do so poorly? What if you're self-abusive or self-destructive? And what if you reject notions of a stable 'self'? Loving people raises a range of questions about what constitutes their well-being. Since people's needs and desires are not static, but open to change, caring for others should involve developing a rich sense of what's important to them, by maintaining an interest in what their needs and desires are. However, it can be incredibly difficult to understand one's own motivations, desires, or the reasons we act in certain ways. So, it's fair to assume that we cannot be sure what's in other people's heads or hearts, since our experiences, understandings and practices of love are diverse, complex, fluid and multitudinous.

Labours of love

Those who view love as a form of weakness fail to appreciate how caring connections can transform social conditions. Love can be based on hopeful practices and strategies that recognise both the limits and potentials of our relationships. Many people overemphasise the negativity of the world and seek to ruthlessly criticise everything. This is often because they fail to account for the positive impact of love and ignore how the work of love, care and solidarity, reproduce positive developments. Yet it is true that capitalist social relations restrict how and whether we can love – limiting what we can do and what we can be, damaging our personalities, cutting us off from each other and our potentials, giving rise to numerous internal and external obstacles to love. Importantly we must continue to grapple with how some people's professed love for themselves, their community, ethnicity, identity, or nation, can involve the hatred of others.

It is widely recognised and understood that the most important contributor to the development of a child is love – their progress is largely dependent on whether they are cared for, whether those around them, their 'carers', love them. So, if the presence or absence of love is the most important aspect in the development of an individual, it is likely the same can be said for all social development. In my previous writing, I've explored how the language of love can discipline us to obey, work and consume. What we do with our time, and what we work to produce, are vital considerations. As the distinction between 'work' and 'non-work' becomes hazier, questions are frequently raised about what 'work' is? what should we do with our time? and what should we love? Increasingly we're supposed to love what we do and find our passions in work. Yet many of us find our paid jobs less and less fulfilling.

A major obstacle when discussing 'work' is that the term tends to be limited to the re/productive work of and for capital and neglects the work of constructing living alternatives – the work of love. Love

Nick Southall and Sharon Pusell at *Love 2014*. Photo by Ella Pusell.

is an achievement; it is something we create, both individually and collectively. Yet love can be hard work. If we're not prepared for our loving relationships to include struggles with pain and sorrow, and to provoke anxieties and fears, to at times involve loneliness, disappointment, vulnerability and fragility, then we're ill prepared for love. These normal characteristics of loving relations do not negate love, sure they can make loving more difficult, but pure love is a fantasy. The idea that as a couple we become one person, or that our significant other is 'the one' we're destined to be with, can be torn asunder when we find that we can't fully understand them, they don't understand everything about us, and there's a lot we don't have in common. John Armstrong explains it is therefore 'extremely important to work with a vision of love which sees problems not as the end of love, not as a sign that love is over, but as the ground upon which love operates.'

Most of us want love to last and be able to withstand the difficulties long-term relationships bring with them. My partner, Sharon, and I have been together for 35 years and we both agree that developing and maintaining such an enduring bond is a difficult endeavour. As Sharon explained in her speech at our 25th anniversary party, our love is a shared effort –

Nick and I decided to call this party a 'celebration of love' because we wanted to not only celebrate our years together, but also celebrate and say thank you to all of you, our family and friends, for the love, support and friendship we've received over those years. When we started thinking about what to do to mark this date, some people suggested that we really should do something romantic together as a couple, rather than have a big party. But we understand and appreciate that it is your love which has made our love possible. So, this celebration is a celebration of all of our love.

Learning to love

It is widely understood that the labours of love are disproportionately borne by women, most of which is unpaid, with the value, power, and influence of this work under-estimated. At the same time, many people believe that sacrificing their lives to stultifying work is an act of love for the family they're meant to provide for. We tend to surrender much of our lives – minute by minute, day by day, year by year – to the competitive and often hard-hearted pursuit of 'making a living'. Working for a boss or a bureaucracy, competing with others in a ruthless struggle to 'get ahead', undermines our ability to love, leaving too little time or energy for what is most important – those we love and learning the art of loving.

'Love isn't to be sought after, it's everywhere,
and to search is self-deception,
a charade.' – Leo Buscaglia

Caring for others continually involves overcoming obstacles, as we work on overcoming these obstacles, we learn how to cultivate the growth and development of our loving power. Learning to love involves conscious decisions to change what we do and to take the time necessary to mould new ways of living and being. In his book *The Art of Loving*, Erich Fromm argues that love is an art and learning this art can be divided into two parts: theory and practice. Love requires a great deal of practice, and theoretical knowledge and the results of practice need to be blended together– what is often called praxis. But, according to Fromm, there's a third factor necessary for learning any art — it should be a matter of ultimate concern – and here lies the answer to why people struggle to learn the art of love. Despite a deep-seated craving for love, almost everything else tends to be considered more important: a job, career, success, prestige, money, possessions, etc. According to Fromm, love is the only thing that can fully connect us to another person – and since he believes that being disconnected from other people is the central problem of our times, love is the solution to the key problem of human existence. Here the problem is not one of finding a person to love, but in developing our capacities to care for others – to love them. Searching for the right 'object' diverts attention from these tasks.

Learning to love involves adapting our subjectivities – changing our perceptions, our priorities and our behaviours. To give more time to love, and to connect loving theory and practice, the Love collective has continued to hold regular discussions about various readings related to love. We've looked at the commodification of love and the need to transform work, explored questions about whether, or how, to work for wages, and in what ways the power of love has played a part in social struggles and movements. A while ago, we read 'Social reproduction: between the wage & the commons' an interview with Silvia Federici on the importance of care work; for people, relationships, communities and social movements. Federici uses the example of Greece, where capital and its state forms are in deep crisis, to highlight the networks of social solidarity and support which have been organised to help people survive and to create living alternatives to capitalism. She also discusses the leading role of women in creating these alternatives, arguing that while wages and wage struggles remain important these need to compliment struggles to expand our autonomy from capital, and to reappropriate the wealth we create.

Exploring the importance of love to social reproduction, the Love reading group has considered the situation of many care workers, such as nurses, educators, etc., who are dissatisfied with their paid work because they cannot do a decent job due to constant cuts, erosion of working conditions, casualisation and the continual re-organisation of their work, which erodes the social relations between those who care/are cared for. This, of course, reflects a more general pattern where caring relationships (family ties, friendships, etc.) are undermined. Via another reading ('Bridging the worlds of therapy & activism: intersections, tensions & affinities') we've looked at the difficulties of 'working in accordance with our ethical stance' and how going against this stance causes us pain. This article highlights the importance of believing our work matters, that what we do makes a positive difference. Yet, the authors ask, how can our usefulness be measured? Their answer is – it cannot. However, the value of what we do can be indicated by other people, when they acknowledge its worth. Therefore, they argue, we need 'solidarity teams' to help nurture and support us, to remind us of our ethics, and so we can work in constructive cooperative collaborations. These 'solidarity teams' may include family, work mates, friends, allies, and even people we've never met (e.g. for me bell hooks or Joe Strummer can be on my team).

Loving solidarity

There's a growing need for the collective organising of affective politics and various forms of 'solidarity teams' can provide times/spaces where we develop reciprocal caring relationships. Over the last few years, one of my most important 'solidarity teams' has been the Love collective. Together we sustain and support each other, offer camaraderie, and help to provide hope. We also learn about how other people are trying to do the same, reading articles like 'The street syndicate: re-organising informal work' by Carlos Delclos which focuses on the struggles of informal workers in Barcelona and the need to organise this work collectively, with the aim of putting human dignity above property rights. Carlos explores various perspectives on the 'informal economy' and considers how the 'sharing economy' can both reinforce capitalist exploitation and provide mutual aid. Importantly he also highlights how Barcelona's African and unemployed communities take care of each other through self-organisation and group solidarity.

Another article that struck a chord among the reading group, and among others who talked about it on social media, was 'Life-hacks of the poor & aimless'

Drawing by Siobhan Christian.

by Laurie Penny. She examines several issues raised during the group's previous discussions, including the problem of activist burn-out, the importance of taking care of yourself and others, and the relationship between self-care/individual fulfilment and collective engagement/social solidarity. Laurie points out that queer and feminist communities understand the personal is political and that 'real love' is an action rather than just a feeling. Commenting on Facebook, in a heart-felt response to this text, one of our friends explained how she had countered her own anxiety through contributing to the community and by reconnecting to her political ideals via engaging in collective struggle. Recent social movements, such as Love Makes a Way or Equal Love, reflect similar understandings and seek to deploy love politically. Inspired by the Equal Love campaign, the Love reading group discussed 'The meaning of love in the debate for legal recognition of same-sex marriage in Australia' by Renata Grossi. This article revolved around the need to pose the marriage equality campaign as a struggle about love in order to counter the restriction of love to heterosexual relationships, to help transform social perceptions of love, and to demonstrate the power of mobilising love. It concluded by arguing that we need to redefine love 'in a way that retains its utopian ideals' and expresses 'love's optimism.'

What is love?

Some of you may have read this piece looking for a simple, complete theory of love; a pithy answer to the question posed, rather than ideas suggesting the richness and varieties of love and the wide-ranging debates and activities currently spreading around the world. Narrow notions of love limit our imaginations and horizons, while open and expansive conceptions of love both challenge us and indicate how our social encounters and collaborations can bring us joy. The purpose of the Love collective and the *Love: Art, Ideas, Music, Politics* festivals is to foster continuing dialogue and encounter. We interpret our theme broadly and are interested in conversations that celebrate love's power and share collectively in an exploration of its meaning. Rather than providing definitive answers – we prefer to carry on discussing and debating various forms of love, their uses and usefulness – constructing a range of responses as we 'learn to love by loving'. Recognising that love is a form of power produced by our efforts to create alternative relationships and community, we seek to develop grounded optimism and realistic hope for the future, as we continue to ask – what is love?

Let Us Meet by the River: Love as Regeneration
Annette Maguire

Justice is what love looks like in public.
  – Cornel West

We are either going to have a future where women lead the way to make peace with the Earth, or we are not going to have a human future at all.
  – Vandana Shiva

As I write, the Amazon burns. The fires are on a scale enormous enough to be visible from space, engulfing much of the ancient rainforest that provides 20% of the oxygen our planet relies on. Brazil's president, the openly fascist Jair Bolsonaro, has given a clear signal to agribusiness and other extractive industries that Burning Season is on, and they can eliminate as much of the Amazon as possible. Hardly a case of 'small farmers', it is, unmistakeably, the usual corporate suspects funding the destruction – including Nestle, Cargill, Walmart, and of course McDonalds. More importantly, while they do so, these interests are literally stealing the vast ancestral lands of Indigenous peoples (including no less than 350 distinct nations), as well

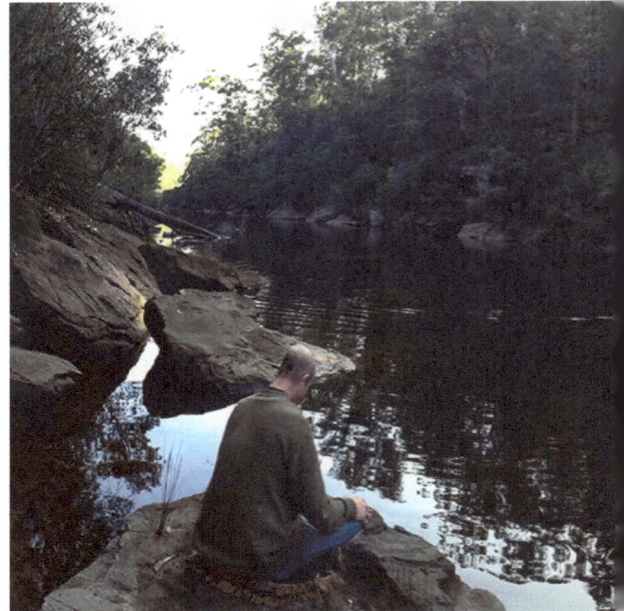

as territories reclaimed by landless workers through social struggles. As such, they are displacing and exterminating the millions of Indigenous and landless workers who live there. These are the very people who have been caring for the Amazon – regenerating the oxygen we all rely on, resisting the extractive assault of corporations on the jungle through the decades, and regenerating their communities to make sure these practices are passed on. The emperor wears no clothes: here is patriarchal colonial capitalism exposed in all it's grotesque nakedness: obliterating the 'lungs of the world' while simultaneously perpetrating mass murder and genocide, right in this present moment.

I open with this dark picture, because the contrast between that which murders en masse, and that which generates life could not be more stark. The far-right surge around the world means that capitalism is only going to look more like Bolsonaro. Yet power doesn't flow only from above, but also from below. We can tap a wellspring of enormous potency if we so choose. To powerfully resist capitalism, and keep ourselves in one piece while we are at it, we need to learn how to resist and how to regenerate more like the Indigenous women of the Amazon. They have been resisting colonial capitalism and its practices of genocide and ecocide for more than five hundred years. At the absolute centre of this is care. No one gets chucked in the bin, and everyone contributes to the care of the whole. We need to have the humility to start doing our activism and our lives the way Indigenous women do, guided by indigenous ways of being, knowing, and doing. Noam

Indeed, so vital has their caring work been for human flourishing, that a growing body of scientific knowledge now backs the Grandmother Theory. This theory argues that grandmothers were crucial to human evolution itself, helping us develop social skills, more sophisticated brains, and capacities for co-operation. Yet the figure of the Grandmother couldn't be further from the image we have of the 'heroic activist', who is coded as young, male and fairly aggressive, as befits the warrior stereotype. Meanwhile, occasional thank-yous aside, the deep marginalisation of grandmothers and older women in this society is clear from a glance at the runaway rates of homelessness, poverty and loneliness besetting their (our) lives.

Participants take a break by the river, *Love 2014*. Photo by Justin Westgate.

Chomsky has said that Indigenous women will save the planet. But that's only part of the equation. Frankly, Indigenous women are not going to do our work for us, they certainly won't save us if we are not doing our part. There is no room for carrying on with business as usual, nor even eco-business as usual, let alone activism as usual – this will not enable us to save the planet or each other.

Only by radically reorganizing our lives and activism along the lines of care can we hope to get there. So what would that look like in our own lives, in the here and now? I want to propose that, closer to home, what that looks like is learning to be more like the people who repair and maintain life. Closer to home, the people who enact love as regeneration are, above all, older women. Aboriginal older women most of all. Because older women are the world class experts in this area.

Nonetheless, many of the most crucial social struggles over the decades have been led by older Aboriginal women. These include the campaign for land rights – led among others by the legendary Mum Shirl; the winning struggle against the Jabiluka mine on Mirrar country; the fight against the radioactive waste dump at Muckaty Station; the DjabWurrung struggle for country underway as we speak; and in NSW, the struggle by Grandmothers Against Removals against the state's creation of new stolen generations. Moreover, unofficial grandmothers who don't have biological children themselves often perform this same kind of vital justice work and caring work.

Embodied politics: situating myself

As a woman over forty, I feel myself entering this demographic of older women, and feel the invisibility and precarity that go with it. As a queer warrior woman, I have given my life to organising for social justice, and paid a high price for doing so (I regret nothing). Consequently I occupy a very marginal position in the labour market, have lived on a low income for 25 years, and have no personal wealth for my retirement. However, as a single woman over 40 I have learned thoroughly how to care for myself and how to repair, heal, and regenerate. Therefore, I know how to do these vital acts for others too. I am an active presence in my small housing co-operative, where for six years I have been a maintainer and repairer, not of physical buildings, but of ongoing group capacities and relationships. The role I fulfil is seldom visible and rarely valued, but it is the kind of work that concretely makes it possible to live in a way that is kinder to people and planet, in a model that can be replicated infinitely. But it definitely doesn't fit the family-centric imagery of love and care we are accustomed to (and that is endlessly drummed into us in the media spectacle – from Disney to most TV shows).

Is it so outrageous to believe that in order to save the planet, it wouldn't hurt for people to do a bit more of what I do, and for it to become visible? Yet as noted, my labours of love and care are devalued. Not for any personal reasons, but for structural ones. These labours are traditionally women's work, and that work is devalued. This gets to a crucial sticking point when it comes to championing love as a political project. When it is women who are doing the loving, it is invisible because it is expected of us to love, as a matter of duty. Indeed, the entire capitalist economy depends absolutely on the unpaid caring work of women, a form of extractivism applied to our feminised bodies en masse. The designated role of woman as helpmate, caring as a condition of our existence, may well be outdated, but it is a role that is relentlessly resurrected and re-imposed by a capitalism mired in a structural crisis that it seeks to solve by foisting the ever-expanding labours of care onto women's backs. This also creates a conundrum of how to resist capital's extraction of our care, given we have been conditioned to see giving care as our core purpose in life, and when we face a massive backlash if we refuse to give.

But I would argue that this is precisely why it is so urgent to retrieve the shining kernel within care from its capitalist shell, and restore its authentic and immeasurable value, by making care the touchstone of our lives and resistance. This would mean displacing the traditional framing of politics as 'war by other means', where dehumanized patriarchal male 'warriors'

cockfight and crush the loser; to politics as love, as the affirmation and regeneration of life enacted by fierce and tender co-operating feminised warriors of love. As an image and archetype of this unglamorous but life-affirming model, the illustrious feminist poet Marge Piercy writes in *Let Us Gather at the River*:

I mend old rebellions and patch them new.

In her poem, Piercy offers a utopian vision, but one that is firmly rooted in this world, this earth, and is not starry-eyed about the violence that confronts us and harms us, and which we can resist if we continue to heal and repair as we resist.

Love and its opposite: differentiating love from violence

Recent decades have seen an enormous rise in disability and chronic illness in Western countries, yet these are largely viewed as individual problems. In a world that is brutally violent, disability is inextricably bound up with trauma and grief. The social model of disability, created by disabled folks themselves, shows that disability is in fact produced by the ableism of a capitalist society that reduces people to their performance in a cut-throat labour market. Any barriers to access people experience are seen as irrelevant 'externalities' that the individual disabled person is responsible for bridging on their own. The minimal access adjustments we see in daily life are a drop in the ocean and the outcome of fierce struggle by disabled people over many decades (as depicted, for example, in the film *Defiant Lives*). Moreover, illness, trauma and disability are seen as abject, shameful and a deficit. This is not wiped away by trendy 'inspiration porn' that reduces disabled persons to cheery, inspiring mascots who can make abled people feel better about themselves. What if we saw trauma and disability as a resource of wisdom and strength rather than as a deficit? And even more radically, what if we understood care not as 'support', but as mutual aid. That is, mutual aid both in the sense of reciprocity – mutual giving and receiving – but also as an act of caring that itself gives back to the carer? The path-breaking Marxist feminist Selma James, who founded the international Wages for Housework movement, argues that care is a fundamentally self-civilising act – learning to put someone else before oneself is a profound learning that civilises the self in a way that selfish grasping (as perfected by the universal male subject, for example) never can.

A lot of violence has been and continues to be done in the name of 'care' and 'support'. What is love and care? We often see it as situated in the family. What happens, then, for people like me for whom the family is the site of violence? Melinda Cooper has written on the push back to the nuclear family enacted by the neoliberal powers that be over the past 30-odd years. She shows how central the family values ideology is to the neo-liberal project, and a direct backlash towards the opening up of relationships and kinship models unleashed by the mass social struggles of the 1960s-70s, especially feminism and LGBT liberation. The forced re-confinement of the site of welfare to the family and the offloading of the responsibility of state and society in this arena that we see under neoliberal capitalism is a very real threat to the lives of enormous numbers of people. However, to attempt to name this form of dispossession is to be demonised in the interests of maintaining the mythology of the sanctity of the nuclear family.

Care has been co-opted into the much-hyped, harmful mystique of self-care. Care has been reduced to its more public-relations friendly, pretty-face component of middle-class nuclear families raising children. The soft-focus romanticisation of mothers raising children has always been a colossal hypocrisy and yet caring for family members is being pushed onto women within the family thanks to the smashing of the welfare state. The semi-visibilised forms of care cover up the so-called dark side – and it is spoken of in these terms even by those who apparently value it – of disability, illness, poverty. This side is never romanticized through a soft-focus lens, but is always demonized as ugly, unsightly, unromantic, lonely, atomised. Part of the reason for this is its secret, potent power. If more people valued and engaged in this care, they might come to love the vulnerability in themselves and others, to view vulnerability with tenderness and no longer be willing to engage in the cutthroat competition this society demands of us daily. What would become of society and inequality if people began to love the abject? The rejected and despised? The demonised?

Gender violence is very strongly indicated in health issues for women and is the leading cause of illness, disability and death for women aged 15–45. The expectation on women to provide care is violent. The confinement of love to the nuclear family is violent. It is very common to experience family as a prison and a domestic slavery, yet we are demonized for speaking about it as such. To work upon and redress this matrix of micro and macro violences requires intricate reparative labours. We need to work in slow time, over time. Love as a doing word. The labours of love in which the personal is political and the political is personal, are conducted over the long haul. They are not fickle and fleeting. As Selma James says, invest in caring not killing. Recently the first march of Amazon Indigenous women danced its way through the streets of Brazil's capital, and several of the women said: 'it is through communal life that a dignified life can be sustained'.

Burn, Australia, Burn

John Passant

The Love Collective would like to pay our respects to John who died just before this book went to press. John was a lifelong socialist and fighter for social justice. We are grateful for his performance of his poems at Love 2017 *with his friends from the band* The Awesome *and for giving us this poem to include in the book.*

Vale John Passant.

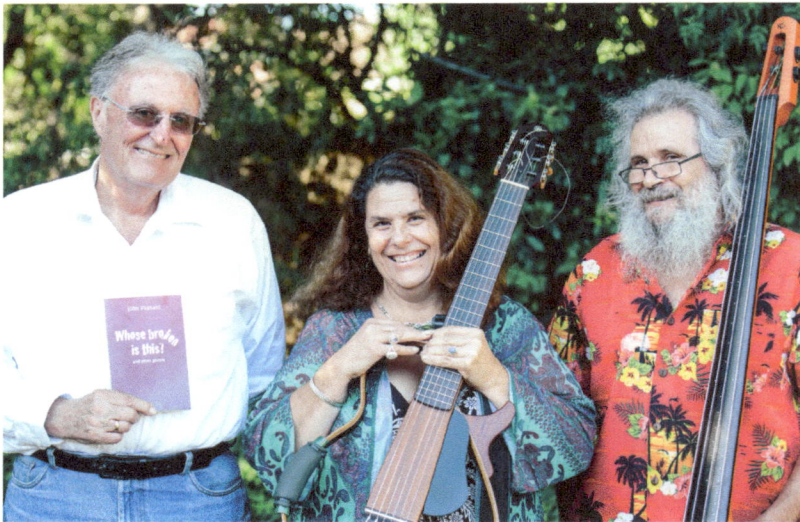

The Awesome
(feat. John Passant).
Photo by Gill Davis.

Burn in your sun
My country, beloved, begone
Burn like you did
The people here
When you arrived
They died
Burnt souls
Sent from their soils
Their land
Your spoils

Burn your anger
Over poems of the burned
The damned who fought back
You have burnt destruction
Into their today
Go away, burners
Let the burned speak
And cry, their beloved land

Watch the fire erupt
Against the corrupt
Not just the burners
But their furnace
A land built on fire
A fire that destroyed millions
For the millionaires
No one cares
Except we do
Burn, you bastards, burn
We are coming for you
Men and women grown rich
On stolen land
And the labour of the millions
This will be the cleansing fire
Of our right and ire
A new world awaits
And you are in our way
Burn, your Australia, burn
Ours awaits

Burn, Australia, burn
For the seeds throw the future
Into the ground
And let the new, renewed, grow
A new land
Where love is the tree of life
And all live well
Not the hell of today
But a new way
Burn, Australia, burn

(January 30, 2018)

Photo by Gill Davis.

Anti-colonial Affections: How Migrants Might Spurn White Australia's Demands for Love in Favour of Solidarity With Aboriginal Resistance

Sunil Menon

An affectation of innocence underscores white Australia's relation to non-white migrants who arrive here. It exists as a certainty in the inherent goodness of the structures of liberal democracy, a belief that the welcome that has been given to us migrants is charitable and tolerant in such a way that reinforces a position of benevolent authority. In conjunction with this belief is the sense that non-white migrants are always looking to exploit the naïve kindness of white Australia. This is a continuation of racist, colonial narratives that disguises the violence of colonisation by positioning white people as constantly endangered by the lurking, dangerous brown/black other, who will use any means – barbaric and violent or sneaky and underhanded – to access all the goodness of white society. The sense of fragility and paranoia that these colonial narratives engender mean that migrants' place here is predicated on endlessly demonstrating our gratitude for having been allowed to stay. We are expected to display our affection and attachment in ways that are both recognisable to and uphold the assumed neutrality of liberal democracy by not calling it for what it is: white, liberal democracy. This veil of innocence, of impartiality, attempts to obscure a founding violence that defines all racial politics in this country, while allowing for the ongoing exploitation and dispossession faced by First Nations people.

Workshop discussion.
Photo by Nina Kourea.

The affective demands that are placed upon migrants are implicated in upholding the racial power that whiteness claims across this continent. Instead of orienting a position within so-called Australia towards such load-bearers of colonisation, could migrants seek out the possibilities of a radical and anti-colonial solidarity where we affirm our presence here by turning towards First Nations struggles for sovereignty and self-determination? Rather than assimilating, might we recognise how our sensibilities have become sharpened and resilient through generations of adaptation, through creating new ways to be against and within the historical, social and cultural dislocations that have followed our experiences of colonisation and migration? While acknowledging our position as settlers in this country, might there be some commonality in these experiences of dislocation and resilience that can cohere around an anti-colonial affection?

To try and ground some of the generalised potential intimated in such questions in actual, concrete relations, I will turn my attention to the activity of Anticolonial Asian Alliance (AAA). Somewhere between being a solid, functioning group and a loose network, AAA is an attempt to build a base of solidarity with Indigenous struggles from within migrant and diasporic communities. Most active in Sydney, the group participates in acts of immediate, material support as well as organising around longer-term campaigns. I will draw on my own peripheral participation and observation, as well as in-depth conversations with some of its core members, to suggest that AAA exemplifies what such a pivot towards Aboriginal custodianship could begin to look like for non-white migrants. It should be noted that while the generalised migrant position that I am referring to is useful as a rhetorical device in identifying racial power dynamics, relations of class and gender, migratory histories and residency/visa status mean there are myriad ways that migrants experience access to institutional power, are able to feel a sense of belonging, or make political choices.

Coerced affection and colonial complicity

'They screaming, 'love it or leave it',
I got more right to be here, if you could believe it.
Won't salute a constitution or who's underneath it.'
– A.B. Original, 'January 26th'

The social and political institutions of white Australia emotionally and structurally coerce non-white migrants into assimilating towards its expectations. Our affection is required to be bestowed upon the structures of the coloniser state, and the cultural symbols and values that uphold it. This is captured in the pre-eminence of the nationalist demand to 'love it or leave it', whether viewed as a bumper sticker on the back of a ute, alongside an image of the Australian flag, or delivered from the pages of the national media. It is a statement bursting with aggressive insistence that migrants display a gratitude for being here that validates white Australia. This is an ultimatum imbued with an indignant belief that such a wholesome, innocent welcome has been given that we are obliged to reciprocate with love. Corresponding to the demand for love, the 'leave it' clause contains a glaring reminder that the place of migrants here is always contentious, capable of being condemned if unable to contort itself to display attachment in ways that satisfy the insecurities of white Australia. Apart from adhering to the political structures and legal apparatus of the state – without calling into question their assumed legitimacy – the assimilation that is expected is emotional, psychological and behavioural, as well as social and cultural. The ensuing, abusive tantrum when this affective reciprocation – that is, assimilation – is not deemed satisfactory, is a hallmark of colonial, patriarchal relations.

While the general effect of the 'love it or leave it' ultimatum might leave first generation migrants feeling compelled to display and re-state their attachment to the host country, this compulsion is worn out when the generations following are expected to do the same. Racial power dynamics in Australia necessarily mean that for migrants to establish any actual sense of purchase, of being here, involves orienting towards white, colonial hegemony. At the same time, that very hegemony ensures a place that will be peripheral. Aileen Moreton-Robinson, a Goenpul writer of the Quandamooka nation, argues in her essay, 'I Still Call Australia Home', that:

> Non-white migrants' sense of belonging is tied to the fiction of terra nullius and the logic of capital because their legal right to belong is sanctioned by the law that enabled dispossession. However, whiteness is the invisible measure of who can hold possession.

Moreton-Robinson's clause that whiteness still determines who holds possession is a crucial, nuanced adjunct in terms of understanding my argument about the material and social position of migrants. However, this position should also be understood as being a part of the colonising process that has facilitated the dispossession of Aboriginal people from country.

In the verse that begins this section, Indigenous hip hop duo A.B. Original assert that they 'got more right to be here'. While it seems ridiculous that two Indigenous mc's would need to do this, it points to how power, affective attachment and the ability to feel at home in Australia is dominated by whiteness. As Moreton-Robinson explains, 'who calls Australia home is inextricably connected to who has possession, and possession is jealously guarded by white Australians'. This jealous and paranoid possessiveness is borne of an ontological crisis, an embedded memory of the illegitimacy of origins – the lie of terra nullius in particular – that permanently destabilises any claims to the validity of white belonging. As part of a continuous struggle against that founding violence and its ongoing manifestations, it makes sense that First Nations people will assert their 'right to be here' or, as Moreton-Robinson does, their 'ontological relationship to land, the ways that country is constitutive of us, and therefore the inalienable nature of our relation to land'. For non-white migrants attempting to assert a place here against the same jealous possessiveness of white Australia, there are a very different set of complications involved.

The complex, contradictory position of migrants within a settler-colonial society partially ensures a complicity in obscuring the founding violence of colonisation and downplaying the ongoing material effects it has in the present. Additionally, our place here affirms the feel-good false narratives of 'tolerance' and 'diversity' within the Australian national imaginary. Ghassan Hage explains that:

> To speak of an Australian memory is not politically innocent. It is part of a hegemonic disposition on the part of the coloniser to complete the integration of the colonised into the reality of the coloniser.

Kenji Khozoei, an active member of AAA, refers to this process of 'integration', as it occurs to migrants, as 'a big fucking gaslighting'. It exists as the pressure to assimilate and contort cultural difference to the service of the 'we' of white Australia. Feminist and race theorist Sara Ahmed noted in a critical analysis of multicultural Australia from 2000, that 'this multicultural nation accepts those differences that do not threaten the 'we' of the Australian being: the differences that cannot be reduced to mere appearance become the *unassimilable*'. While multiculturalism undoubtedly fostered some social changes, it was no actual attempt to transform the underlying base of (racialised, colonial) power. The national imaginary of white Australia – whether the conservative 'land of the fair go' that is tolerant of difference up to a point, or the liberal ideal of the always welcoming, multicultural nation-space – exists on such a narrow precipice between insecurity and historical delusion that no amount of validation can make it feel secure.

French-Algerian anti-colonial writer and activist, Houria Bouteldja, provides a direction to consider how a turn away from white Australia might be framed. While her context is different – migrants in France do not have to consider perpetuating a cycle of colonisation upon the Indigenous people of the country in which they reside – her reflections on building anti-colonial alliances resonate with important lessons for non-white migrants here. She urges that 'we must accept our role in the crime. In euphemistic terms our integration'. As I have argued, this is a crucial first step. However, she also knows that racial power dynamics, combined with our own experiences of colonisation and confronting racism mean that this 'integration' is never complete, that it is always tenuous. Her response emphasises the need to cut entirely against the grain, to reject the comfort of white liberalism, who's 'anti-racism' is predicated on our assimilation without offering any transformative change in racial power structures. Instead, she asks 'what if we took advantage of racism to invent new political horizons? What if we took advantage of 'the failure of integration'? Dare I say that we must even draw some satisfaction from it'? This is a useful point to turn specifically towards Anticolonial Asian Alliance and the possibilities of solidarity and affective attachment that their activity brings into play.

Taking responsibility as an act of care and solidarity

'White Australia is not a host, it's a parasite really...'
– Eliza Wright, AAA member

During my conversations with active members of Anticolonial Asian Alliance (AAA), one small anecdote seemed to capture the significance of the work they do in trying to undo the erasure of Aboriginal presence from the lived reality of many migrants. Eliza relayed how a parent of a AAA member had seen one of their posters, where the phrase 'you are on Aboriginal land' is translated into multiple languages. This parent commented that he had never previously thought about how the word 'Aboriginal' would be written in Sanskrit. If the migrant position within white Australia has been complicit in concealing the ongoing material effects of colonisation, it makes sense that an important counter would be to make that reality legible and understood within migrant and diasporic communities. AAA insist that migrants need to take responsibility for their role in the obfuscation of the ongoing colonial reality that Indigenous people face.

AAA member, Suu-Mei Chew, makes the point that 'a lot of migrants will have this thing about giving back… but the way you should be doing that is by addressing yourself towards, and making relationships, with Mob'.

Understanding that the country we are on is not simply 'white Australia', but has traditional Aboriginal owners with historical, cultural and environmental connection to the land, who were violently dispossessed of their custodianship, is crucial in building anti-colonial solidarity. This is something that AAA recognises acutely and works from, with Kenji describing how, 'as Asian migrants, our access to some degree of institutional stability is intentionally at the expense of the original people of this land'. At the same time, AAA's strategy also recognises that migrants often want to give back to the community that they have settled in. Separate to the coerced obligations towards white Australia, this tendency can be considered a positive attribute for fostering social bonds and solidarity. However, it tends to be misdirected, with no recourse given to the history of colonisation in this country and who's actual land we're on. As Eliza goes on to explain:

Why do people like our parents feel the need to give back? And is that a good thing? Well yeah, but it's just about re-routing and re-framing that same concept (giving back) and understanding that this is not white Australia. White Australia is a lie.

This re-routing is partially a question of sharing information. Suu-Mei adds that 'the point of engaging with Asian communities is that a lot of people don't even think about it that way, but if you talk to them, [they'd recognise that] I've been addressing myself to the wrong person'. Shifting the scope of who gets addressed towards Aboriginal sovereignty begins to undermine the presumed right to power of white, colonial institutions.

AAA frame anti-colonial solidarity as a responsibility that migrants should assume as part of navigating their place in this country. Even as it is accepted that migrants occupy a complicated socio-political position in relation to colonisation here, AAA explicitly base their activity on an understanding that like white Australia, they too are settlers on Aboriginal land. This has given the group a focus beyond its origins as a Facebook-based meme page that drew on the idea of a common Asian identity to humorously and politically counter white supremacy. Individual member's participation in campaigns and rallies in support of First Nations' struggles were a precursor to this shift. AAA member, Harry Bonifacio Baughan, recalls that 'there was a fair bit of figuring out why we have to be accountable from a practical reason and a moral reason'. This resulted in a turn towards a more active phase where AAA began to appear as a more noticeably organised presence at rallies such as the annual Invasion Day march. They also became more involved in supporting other Indigenous campaigns, organising from alongside, and within, the group F.I.R.E. (Fighting In Resistance Equally) – an Aboriginal led group that facilitates involvement and action across a variety of political and social issues. One of the most significant campaigns that AAA have been involved in, is assisting with efforts to provide support to people in Gamilaraay country, in north-western NSW (specifically around the towns of Walgett and Collarenebri) who have no access to safe drinking water due to the environmental crisis that has seen rivers run dry in the region. The practical solidarity that they have contributed has involved fundraising, spreading information about the crisis, as well as participating in the delivery of water and installing water filters in the affected areas.

Further to this political shift, all four participants articulated scepticism about the value of 'identity politics' as an organising principle, suggesting that basing political struggle purely around the commonalities of an 'Asian' identity was insufficient. Eliza made the point that the group 'started to reject what Asian-ness is, in terms of settler-hood'. The problem being that 'Asian-ness' did not account for the material and structural issues of colonisation and exacerbated the problem of making Indigenous struggles invisible. This wasn't outright denying that Asian migrants had experienced structural racism. Instead, it looked to the inter-connection between racism, white supremacy and colonialism. Harry described how ideologically their position became one of 'identifying that the problem is capitalism, identifying that the problem is colonialism, and then acting accordingly'. This recognised migrants' experiences of racism and built from there to assert that another basis of commonality – that came to be seen as more significant – was that all people involved in AAA were settlers in relation to colonisation and Indigenous struggle.

Acknowledging a position as settlers and how this relates to colonisation and structural racism, is an important step towards making migrancy political in a way that does not merely assimilate to white Australia. In ascribing how 'migrants are in a contradictory colonial location', Ghassan Hage argues that 'migration is, in an important sense, a continuation of the colonisation process', but also that 'they [migrants] are quite capable of relating to Australia's history from the imaginary 'we' of the colonised'. He concludes by adding that ''becoming responsible'… might just as well mean contributing to a struggle for Aboriginal sovereignty'. Confronted by the racism of white Australia, finding commonalities with Indigenous struggle would not only be an imperative for migrants to take responsibility, but become something of a solution to the psychological toll of race dynamics in Australia. Kenji suggests that 'if you're an Asian person in this country and you're sad because people are racist towards you, it's kind of logical that you end up in this (Aboriginal, anti-colonial) struggle'. That is, 'taking responsibility' might not only be framed in relation to Indigenous dispossession and colonisation, but also be about migrants finding an active direction for the resentment that arises from incessantly having to prove attachment and belonging to white Australia. The alliances that are formed in doing so can be a base for acting against the damage of colonisation and white Australia.

AAA's efforts in enacting solidarity with Indigenous struggles has seen them form close working relationships with a number of Aboriginal activists involved in these campaigns. Harry recounts that Aboriginal activists have generally received the presence of AAA at rallies and organising spaces very generously, telling him that 'you (AAA) belong here in the struggle, because our struggles our parallel'. This *is* a generous appraisal, an invitation that we might find common cause due to some crossover in our experiences of racism in this country. As an invitation it stands in stark opposition to the insistence of 'love it or leave it' – instead of a threatening ultimatum it carries the potential of a recognition of each other that can be forged through active struggle and solidarity. As Traditional Owners who have faced the violence of more than two centuries of colonisation, there should be no expectation of such an extension of welcome. However, simply in facing some degree of the racism of white Australia, there are certain relatable experiences that can be a point of connectedness. As Eliza explains 'there are real consequences (of racism) that people who aren't white will understand to a degree'. As such, taking responsibility for our place as non-white migrants and settlers presents an opportunity to put our own experiences of racism and colonialism to use through acting in direct solidarity with Aboriginal campaigns.

Possibilities (or making nightmares a reality)

'I also think in terms of fighting white supremacy, it's just a lot of racist white people's worst nightmare.'
– Harry Bonifacio Baughan, AAA member

The existence and activities of Anticolonial Asian Alliance only begin to suggest at the possibilities which might exist as migrants come to understand their place here as being on Aboriginal land and therefore acting in solidarity with First Nations' struggles for sovereignty. Such a move begins to undermine the coherence of the national imaginary of the racist, colonial state and the symbols and values that uphold it. In rejecting the conditional 'welcome' of this country on anti-colonial grounds, migrants would help to expose the founding violence at its core and the lie in its appearance of neutral, liberal benevolence. As Harry alludes to, even early manifestations of such formations are 'racist white people's worst nightmare'. This is not to suggest that these alliances are on the verge of forming broadly in such a way that will overturn the colonial structures of white Australia. For migrants to claim responsibility for their complex and contradictory social location requires a re-routing of attempts to create a place here away from the institutions and expectations of white Australia and towards Aboriginal sovereignty. This would involve questioning what it means to even 'create a place' on colonised land. These are difficult questions, yet they also point to the significance of AAA – that just before such thoughts become too abstract or seem too far away, they are a real, grounded example of what it is to start acting upon them. Partaking in anti-colonial solidarity with Indigenous struggles holds the potential to open a space for migrants to establish new forms of affective attachments that reject white Australia's insecure demands for love and validation. Instead of trying to fulfil such demands, there can be a taking of responsibility for conflicted emotions and positions, for tensions that might even be unresolvable, that might lead us to finding a basis of anti-colonial commonality, care and affection.

Men in Love workshop at
Love 2017
Photo by Nina Kourea.

I Hope You Like It

Paul Spencer

This love I have for you I hope you like it though it's most-ly second – hand, But I

cleaned it up like new, and I wrapped it in a love–ly rubber band, And it's

from so man–y plac – es, so you may de–tect some trac – es of the

way that it's been passed from hand to hand, I hope you'll un –

– der – stand.

2. When we quietly sit together, that's a love my brother gave me long ago,
   Though I'm floating like a feather, it's a love that doesn't have to be on show,
   And when I treat you as a team-mate, and I tell you every dream I have,
   I learnt that from my sister first you know,
   Such a gift she did bestow.

3. Some simple praise to save me, that's a love I got once from a high-school friend,
   Or the love my Grandma gave me, that I'm giving back to her now till the end,
   I could name so many others, all my family, friends and lo-overs,
   Who gave me all this love I've got to spend,
   And to share with you, my friend.

4. So when you're struck with sadness and you're sulking like we all can sometimes do,
   And I know it would be madness, if I start being cross and grumpy too,
   Then if sometimes I remember, not to close down in a temper,
   But to speak the love that underneath is true,
   That's a love I learnt from you.

Reflections On Love and Struggle

John Rainford

Many will call me an adventurer – and that I am, only one of a different sort – one of those who risks his skin to prove his truth ... I have loved you very much, only I haven't known how to express my affection. I am extremely rigid in my actions, and I think that sometimes you didn't understand me. It hasn't been easy to understand me. Nevertheless, please take me at my word today ... An abrazo (hug) from your obstinate and prodigal son.

– Che Guevara, 31 March, 1965

So wrote Che Guevara in a farewell letter to his parents in Argentina following his decision to lead a group of Cuban revolutionaries on a mission to the Congo to assist the Congolese liberation movement. The letter was written in Havana prior to his secret departure. It was not until October 1965 when news of his leaving was made public. Shortly before his departure, his mother, Celia de la Serna de la Llosa, knowing she was ill, had asked to see him. But, as Che wrote, 'it hadn't been possible for me to go, as preparations for my trip were already far advanced'. It was a letter his mother never read. She died on 19 May 1965. The lonely day in the Congo when Che received the news of his mother's death was said to be the saddest of his life.

Che Guevara had a profound love for his family, even though he struggled to express it to his parents. His love of 'living humanity' was as profound as it was eloquently expressed. On March 12 1965, an article of Che's, *From Algiers to Marcha*, was published in Montevideo, Uruguay. It was here that his famous words about love and revolution first appeared:

> At the risk of seeming ridiculous, let me say that the true revolutionary is guided by great feelings of love. It is impossible to think of a genuine revolutionary lacking this quality. Perhaps it is one of the great dramas of the leader that he or she must combine a passionate spirit with a cold intelligence and make painful decisions without flinching. Our vanguard revolutionaries must idealise this love of the people, one of the most sacred causes, and make it one and indivisible. They cannot descend, with small doses of daily affection, to the level where ordinary people put their love into practice.

> The leaders of the revolution have children just beginning to talk, who are not learning to say 'daddy'; their wives, too, must be part of the general sacrifice of their lives in order to take the revolution to its destiny. The circle of their friends is limited to the circle of comrades in the revolution. There is no life outside it.

> In these circumstances one must have a large dose of humanity, a large dose of a sense of justice and truth in order to avoid dogmatic extremes, cold scholasticism, or an isolation from the masses. We must strive every day so that this love of living humanity is transformed into actual deeds, into acts that serve as examples, as a moving force.

Apologising to your parents for not knowing how to express your love for them during the difficult time of adolescence would seem to be an act of love in itself. It is, perhaps, something that many have felt. All the more so if it wasn't said before the untimely death of a parent. But if expressing a love of humanity was risking ridicule in 1965, it soon became associated with rebellion.

On 14 January 1967, some two years after Che's essay appeared, there was a Human-Be-In at Golden Gate Park, San Francisco, where 25,000 people celebrated love and peace and looked forward to the coming Summer of Love.

Che was executed in Bolivia on 9 October 1967. Less than a fortnight later, 75,000 peace protesters surrounded the Pentagon, sticking daisies down the gun barrels of guarding soldiers and proclaiming that 'Che lives'. The slogan of the time was 'Make Love, Not War'. It was accompanied by the resurgence of a movement for 'Free Love'.

What appears above was part of my essay, 'Love and Revolution', published in *Links International Journal of Socialist Renewal*. It was inspired by a speech given by Nick Southall to the 2010 Resistance national conference held at the Railway Institute Hall in Thirroul. I was one of those in the packed audience listening to Nick that Saturday night. About three years later we were both part of the reading love collective organised by Alexander Brown at the University of Wollongong where Alexander was studying. Together with a small group of other people interested in exploring the concept of love, we then became part of the organising committee that went on to stage the *Love: Art, Ideas, Music, Politics* gathering in Minto in April 2014 and the second love gathering in April 2017 in Wollongong.

The 'Love and Revolution' essay formed the basis of a workshop that I presented at Minto. It was a well-attended event that, in the short time available tended to concentrate on the meaning of love. I've long had an interest in the same question.

Despite always having a number of decent dictionaries in my home library, I refused for many years to look at the definition of love, preferring instead to work it out myself, or at least try to do so. It had long been clear to me that there were different types of love besides the ubiquitous 'romantic' love that most of us have probably grown up with.

So what is love anyway? The *Oxford Thesaurus* lists 78 synonyms for the noun love: affinity, care, rapport, harmony, brotherhood, sisterhood, and fellow-feeling among them. The *Macquarie Dictionary* has six different categories of love embracing romantic love, love of close family and friends, and love as a strong predilection or liking, as in love of books. The Ancient Greeks could find three major categories of love, *Eros* (romantic Love) *Philia* (reciprocal Love between friends), and *Agape* (caring for and seeking the best for others), although it must be said that they had no chocolate or AFL football to love.

As a long-time socialist revolutionary I have, as a matter of praxis, been particularly interested in the reciprocal love that comes from shared political activity. And while my own experience has its obvious limitations, it does lead me to conclude that love forged in the heat of struggle can stand as a category of its own.

John Rainford at *Love 2014*. Photo by Ella Pusell.

The main organisers of the two love gatherings that we managed to put together were a small group of people, six of whom were known to me through previous collaboration and past struggles.

I first met Nick Southall and Sharon Pusell in 1998. Although I had been living in Wollongong for nearly ten years by this time, I did not have strong links to the community beyond a group of like-minded people in Scarborough who came together to save the Coledale Hospital and attempt to improve the flood mitigation program for the area.

John Rainford and Sharon Pusell at *Love 2014*. Photo by Ella Pusell.

industrial campaign in Port Kembla several years earlier that was concerned with securing jobs. It was a stitch-up from the start. Eric was alleged to have committed his crime alongside the legendary Union Secretary, Stan Woodbury. Stan was unable to provide evidence for Eric because, conveniently for the prosecution, he had been dead for some years.

As an ex-official of the Dockers union I actually had the documentary evidence to prove his innocence. But this was a political prosecution, primarily aimed at discrediting the MUA, so it had to be fought both in, and outside, the courts. Through a mutual comrade I was able to arrange a meeting with Nick who readily agreed to help convene a community meeting that kicked off our Free Eric Wicker campaign. A very dear friend from Melbourne with whom I first discussed the notion of love, Peter Ewer, made a film supporting Eric, *Touch One, Touch All* that was screened in Wollongong, Sydney and elsewhere. The national newspaper, *Green Left Weekly*, became a strong supporter of the campaign. A dispute that was previously unknown outside Wollongong was now national news.

When the case came to trial there was a huge crowd of supporters both in and outside the Wollongong courthouse. I was unable to sit in the courtroom as the case proceeded because I was the one (and only) witness for the defence. But sitting outside, I knew it was all over when a huge cheer broke out. It took little more than an hour for the prosecution case to be thrown out and Eric, who was facing a lengthy prison sentence if convicted, left the court a free man. We did not stop there, though. Eric had spent a fortune on legal fees so we went back to court where he was awarded costs. According to the lawyers, this was highly unusual.

There is a real sense of satisfaction in taking on and defeating the federal government and the NSW judiciary. But it could not have happened without the community support that Nick and Sharon were able to organise.

Alexander Brown was in the court that day, not at all conspicuous with his red flag flying high. I met him again at the Revolutionary Action (RA) Christmas party in December 1999 held in Nick and Sharon's garage in Fairy Meadow. I became a supporter of RA but was unable to attend many of its actions because of work in Sydney and interstate. In April 2000, we were together on the Joy Mining Machinery picket line in Moss Vale and at a later factory occupation in support of the Joy workers at Unanderra.

I got to know Melanie Barnes through the Stop CSG Illawarra meetings in Thirroul several years ago, and

The defining political event of 1998 was the waterfront dispute that began in April at Patrick Stevedores container terminals in Melbourne, Sydney, and other ports around the country. History now records that the Maritime Union of Australia were able to defeat the Howard government's attempt to destroy the Union, led by Minister for Industrial Relations Peter Reith. Massive community support for the MUA played a decisive role in the victory.

As this national dispute was unfolding, there was also a dispute in Wollongong involving an ex-official of the Painters and Dockers Union, Eric Wicker, which the reactionary Peter Reith was foolish enough to brag about at a Liberal Party conference in Tasmania. Eric was charged with extortion for his part in an ongoing went on to work with her as a correspondent for *Green Left Weekly* when she was its editor. In May 2014, the film *Radical Wollongong*, which she and I co-produced, was screened to a packed house at the Gala cinema in Warrawong. The film was shown around the country and overseas and won three international prizes.

It would not have been possible to make the film without the encouragement and support of a large group of people in Wollongong. As with all documentary filmmakers we struggled for funding, but when money was tight, there were always enough individuals and groups like the MUA Veterans to help us see the project through to completion.

The love festival organising collective initially met once a month at the Other Words bookshop in Wollongong. One of the festival tasks that we paid particular attention to was the provisioning of fresh, healthy food three times a day for up to 100 participants – no easy task. My views on the importance of this approach were informed by a paper written by Alexander Brown for the Japanese Studies Association of Australia, 'A Society in Which People Demonstrate: Karatani Kojin and the Politics of the Anti-Nuclear Movement'. Alexander's paper described how activist groups in Japan held 'hotpot parties' that became a focal point for people to come together and talk about a variety of topics. Sharing food and drink are ways in which previously atomised individuals can form loose associations with one another that facilitate dialogue and political action.

We attempted to put this into practice, and judging by the number of people who commented on the quality of the menu, we managed to succeed in doing so. An added bonus for me was teaming up again with Alison Jones, whom I first met in the early 1990's when we were both involved in the community struggle to improve the flood mitigation program in Wollongong's northern suburbs.

Love, resistance and revolutionary social change

If a global resistance to neo-liberal capitalism cemented by love is possible, and I think that it is, we can do worse than begin, as Marx did, with the Ancient Greeks who were the subject of his doctoral investigation and led him to conclude: 'philosophers have only *interpreted* the world, in various ways; the point however, is to *change it*'.

In *Anarchism and other Essays*, Emma Goldman relates how, on thousands of occasions, she was asked why she did not spell out how things would operate under anarchism. She replied:

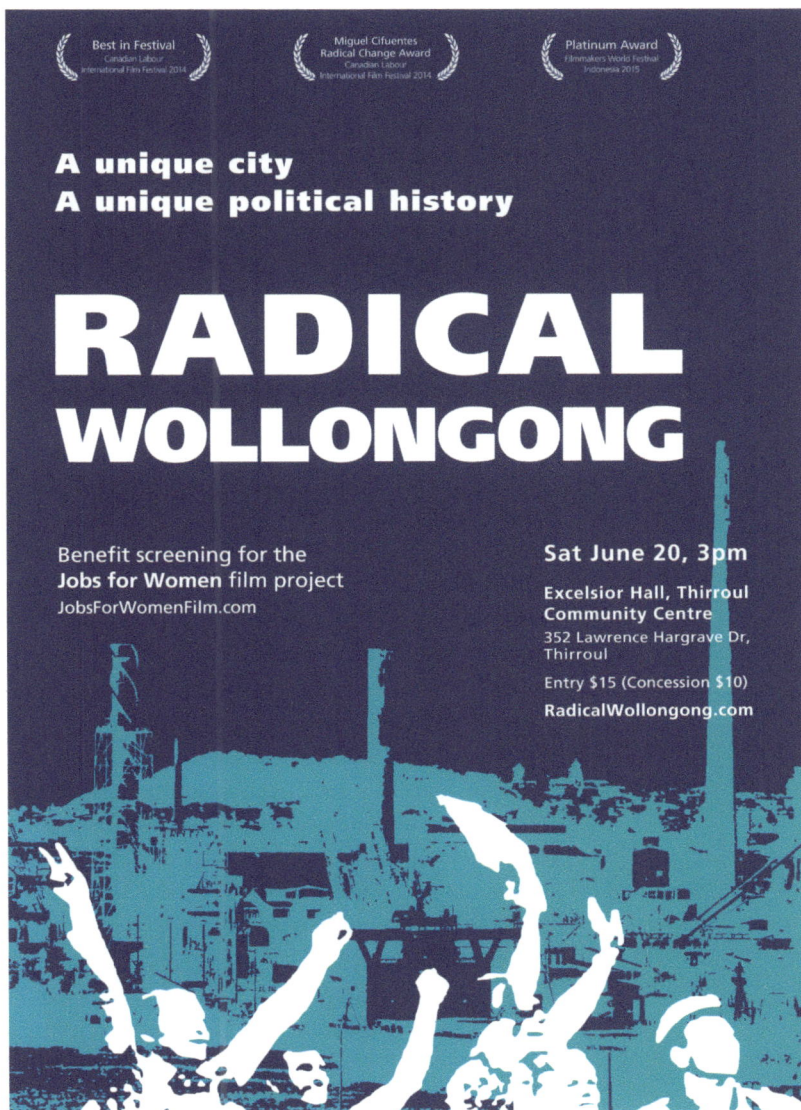

A unique city
A unique political history

RADICAL
WOLLONGONG

Benefit screening for the
Jobs for Women film project
JobsForWomenFilm.com

Sat June 20, 3pm
Excelsior Hall, Thirroul
Community Centre
352 Lawrence Hargrave Dr, Thirroul
Entry $15 (Concession $10)
RadicalWollongong.com

Radical Wollongong poster.
Design by Ash Pemberton.

Because I believe that Anarchism cannot consistently impose an iron-clad program or method on the future. The things that every new generation has to fight, and which it can least overcome, are the burdens of the past, which hold us all in a net. Anarchism, at least as I understand it, leaves posterity free to develop its own particular systems, in harmony with its needs. Our most vivid imagination cannot foresee the potentialities of a race set free from external constraints. How, then, can one assume to map out a line of conduct for those to come? We, who pay dearly for every breath of pure fresh air, must guard against the tendency to fetter the future.'

More than a century on, the burdens of past capitalist production methods that have conquered the world from the time of the industrial revolution now holds us in a net that already threatens the supply of fresh air in many parts of the globe. Anthropomorphic climate change is the inescapable fetter on the future.

In 1842 Marx wrote: 'The fate which a question of the time has in common with every question justified by its content, and therefore rational, is that the question, not the answer, constitutes the main difficulty'. The relevant question of our time has been posed by the Marxist cultural critic, Terry Eagleton:

> One question that therefore arises is how long would it take us to unlearn the ingrained habits of pathological productivity, which after a while acquires a well-nigh unstoppable momentum of its own. Do we have enough time – will an already crippled and wounded Nature give us enough time – for this massive re-education of the senses, the body, the psyche, the disposition of desire itself?

In October 2018, the Intergovernmental Panel on Climate Change (IPCC) provided an answer to Eagleton's question of the time that we have to prevent irreversible climate change that will significantly worsen the risks of drought, floods, extreme heat, and poverty for hundreds of millions of people. Twelve years, according to the world's leading climate scientists, provided that we act immediately.

The existing national and international political structures are almost certainly incapable of achieving this. So what's left? The authors of *Turbulent Transitions* argue that the rise of twenty-first century socialism in Latin America must be located in the context of the collapse of the traditional socialist project:

> In rejecting authoritarianism, bureaucratic centralised planning, state capitalism, and the lack of democracy, it has distanced itself from those traits so common to the failed projects of the twentieth century. A critical attribute of twenty-first century socialism is that it is built by social movements and by people from below; it does not arise from government fiats nor from self-defined vanguard parties. By transforming circumstances, the people transform themselves.

In *Radical Wollongong* we argued that the burden of struggle has shifted from a previously militant, but now emasculated, union movement to civil society. The example that we highlighted was Stop CSG Illawarra, a local social movement built from below that organised three mass actions, each involving more than 3,000 people and that that has so far been able to prevent coal seam gas extraction in our water catchment area. It has also inspired other anti-fracking groups in Australia and beyond.

As the US writer, Rebecca Solnit, wrote following the release of the IPCC report:

> There are so many transformative projects under way from local work to transition off fossil fuels, to the effort to stop pipelines (with some major victories including the one to stop the Trans Mountain pipeline which was won in court late August), to the lawsuit against the US government on behalf of 21 young people charging it with violating their rights and the public trust…we now have the technological capacity to largely leave fossil fuels behind…A revolution is what we need, and we can begin by imagining and demanding it and doing what we can to try and realise it. Rather than waiting to see what happens, we can be what happens.

In short, herculean as the task is, it is not beyond that of living humanity. And at the risk of seeming ridiculous, let me say that it is the love of living humanity that will be decisive in the struggles ahead.

Opposite: Drawing by Siobhan Christian.

Everything Is Something!

Sheryl Wiffen

Sheryl has been travelling to Ziguinchor, Senegal regularly since 2011 and collecting second-hand reading glasses in Australia to be used by the community there. She has also been collecting money, donated by friends, to purchase mosquito nets for people she meets on her visits.

The World Health Organisation estimates that there were 216 million cases of malaria worldwide in 2016 resulting in 445,000 deaths. 91% of these deaths occurred in the WHO African Region There is no vaccine available against this debilitating disease and most of the population cannot afford treatment. The prohibitory cost of mosquito nets makes them unattainable for many families. A $10 donation is enough to purchase a mosquito net impregnated with insect repellant, which provides protection for a mother and her children for up to seven years.

Sheryl Wiffen in Senegal.
Photo by Sheryl Wiffen.

I lay on the double-foam mattress, which I shared with Vicky, musing about this adventure. The foam mattress was naked; no nicely coloured material stretched over the outside. The foam mattress, covered with a cotton sheet, lay on the brown and white tiled floor of our room. I could hear chooks crowing, children crying and adults moving about outside as I lay under the small electric fan, eagerly awaiting its every rotation. The fan created a brief reprieve from the stifling heat and then continued its revolution. I stared at the mosquito net dangling idly from the ceiling. I had borrowed it from a friend in Australia, however after the first night of feeling suffocated under the net, I chose not to use it. The mosquitoes were not bad at this time of year, during the dry season. We burnt mosquito coils and used the insect repellent, which we brought with us. We also had our daily dose of anti-malaria tablets and each morning we reminded each other to take our 'Doxy's'. The mosquitoes were smaller and lighter in colour than the big black mega suckers we were used to in Australia and there was no warning 'bzzzzzzzzzzz' from these silent little malaria-carrying killers. I was bitten but experienced no red swelling or itchy lump under my skin.

Women visit the markets daily. They have no cupboards, refrigerators or containers to store food and cats, mice and rats invade the kitchens at night. Skinny, mangy dogs and cats, feral animals, wandered freely, uncared for. They moved in and out of community spaces, not fierce or scared of humans, surviving on whatever scraps they found. They were just another part of the landscape.

We had planned to go to the morning market with Kade to purchase the new household items, but we woke up too late. We spent the day crouching on our haunches, hand washing our clothes and took turns going to the *gee-bi-o* (well), to draw *gio* (water). We washed dishes, sat in the shade, sang and danced with the children and the women, talking and trying to remember words and listened to various people pick up the guitar.

Our neighbour used red Rosella flowers to make *bissap* juice, which she then turned into delicious, little frozen ice blocks of shear joy. I have no idea how she made ice. The sweet red ice is pronounced 'One Joy' and tastes like it sounds, frozen nectar from the gods. Mariama purchased enough for all of us to enjoy that afternoon.

I saved the watermelon seeds from the fruit we ate the previous afternoon, specifically so we could plant them, thinking it would be a fun experience for the children. I hoped Kade might get involved in

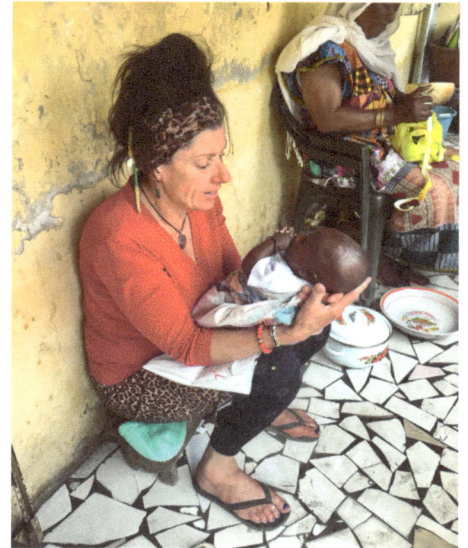

Left: Children and babies are among the most vulnerable to malaria. Right: Midwife Suzy Henderson holding infant in Senegal, 2011. Photos by Sheryl Wiffen.

growing some food but she was not interested at all in this project. A couple of children came bouncing around me, intrigued as I dug a hole with the handle-less broken trowel. I showed them the watermelon seeds, trying to explain what I planned and they told me the name of the fruit is hal or sarou in Mandinka language. We scratched a small area in the sandy soil of the unfinished building's footings, planted the seeds, and watered them with detergent-saturated water from the dishwashing bucket. The seedlings raised their first leaves above the soil within a few days.

I slowly began to remember some people's names as we stopped and chatted briefly with the neighbours when we visited the well. *'Malicoum Salam'* or 'Hello, how are you?' was our chant, which was responded to with *'Salam Malicoum'.* If we had not met the people we greeted at the well, we asked *'No`tudo?'* which means 'What is your name?'

Olivia, our school teacher, encouraged the children, who appeared in our house every day, to write down their names; Mama, Sadidou, Toumani, Fatima, Soudandine, Fatou, Habou, Peuda, Ibrahime, Papa, Afgat, Astou, Afasane. Then we wrote our names on Olivia's notebook as well. An exercise like this took several hours, as every step of the process was enjoyed immensely with laughter and recognition of every letter and name, with much finger pointing to each person in relation to their name.

Women do all the work. They told us of their aches and pains and I felt so lucky to live in a country where we can afford medical attention and basic painkillers such as paracetamol, which was simply out of the reach of the people of Kande Baneto, Ziguinchor. Mariama suggested we form a women's massage circle, however the local women were quite shy so this never eventuated.

We watched the masses of Yellow-billed Kites cruising in circles on the air currents above our heads. Spending time just sitting was foreign to my personal life. I had been a 'doing' sort of person most of my life and this opportunity to just 'be' was gold. It gave me time to observe. As I sat drinking 'Attire' in the shade that afternoon, the littlest Mama brought me a piece of broken red feather. I recognized it immediately as the trinket my daughter tied in my hair before I left Wollongong. Mama held out the red feather and pointed to my hair. I laughed at the sheer ridiculousness of the situation, that a piece of feather had fallen out of my hair. If it had become dislodged anywhere else in my life, very few people would notice it lying on the ground while even fewer would have returned the broken piece to its origin. The incredible barrenness of the landscape snapped my soul awake.

Where there is everything, we can see nothing and where there is nothing, we can see everything. Mama's cheeks spread revealing her perfect white teeth and she laughed with me as I folded her hand around the piece of red feather. Gently stroking her cheek, I gave it back to her with tears in my eyes, unable to communicate the fullness of what I was thinking and feeling. Gestures of affection, love and trust were often our only way of communicating. A lesson in honesty and gratitude from a small piece of red feather that was lost, lying in the dust, and a little girl who had no material possessions.

Love Your Waste

Gavin Moores
and Alexander Brown

One popular art project at Love: Art, Ideas, Music, Politics *was the bread clip mandala. This interactive workshop was facilitated by Gavin Moores and Angie De Santo in 2014 and returned in 2017, when it was facilitated by Gavin Moores. The artists proposed an art project 'using only bread clips and a little help from our friends'. The result in each case was a site-specific mandala installation assembled in real-time during the festivals and photographed before being packed away again at the end of the festival, creating works that were unique to each event in both time and space. In the process, the bread clip project turned a stream of useless waste into a community of people talking and making art. Alexander Brown spoke with Gavin Moores about the project and the ideas behind it.*

Alexander: Gavin, when did you start making bread clip art?

Gavin: When I was house sitting so … nine years ago. No, sorry, when I was in Melbourne, so twelve years ago. A housemate gave his girlfriend a necklace with a silver bread clip on it and that was what triggered me to start collecting bread clips. It was such an ordinary everyday item that you see in your kitchen, you see in the gutter. They manage to clip up all over the place, but this one was made out of silver. I just really liked it so I started collecting with my housemate. I had about 300, he had about 30 and I just kept going.

Alexander: What was the silver bread clip made from? Was it actually silver?

Gavin: Yeah. You can get them on ebay. I'm not sure what inspired him to do that but I really liked it. I thought it was super cute. I was going to start gluing them to an alleyway somewhere in Melbourne and create a bread clip alleyway. There was a bubble gum alleyway where people would get their chewed-up bubble gum and just put it on the brick wall. There was heaps of disgusting chewed up bubble gum in this alleyway. We were going to do a version of that with bread clips, but it never happened.

Alexander: Your first public bread clip piece was part of the Viva La Gong Street Panels Project back in November 2012. What kinds of reactions did you get?

Gavin: Everyone loved it. There were little walking tours of Wollongong street art at the time and it was getting a lot of good reactions from people. There were works by graffiti artists around that were well known. A guy called Rone did an artwork that year and everyone obviously loved his work. He's sort of world famous. People were getting to look at his work alongside mine and they were really loving what I did that year. But I didn't like gluing

Gavin Moores at *Love 2017*.
Photo by Nina Kourea

down the bread clips because I didn't get them back afterwards. I like sweeping up the artwork afterwards and putting them back in jars. The actual gluing down aspect, that was the first and last time I've done that. I didn't like it very much at all. I enjoyed the exhibition and I enjoyed hanging it up, but the process was far from what I normally do.

Alexander: Why do you like to sweep it up afterwards?

Gavin: Because I don't think it looks that good. If you glue it down and hang it up as an art piece it gathers

dust, it gets old, pieces fall off and I just don't like it. It gives you time to pick it apart and really look at the flaws. It's more about the process of making it. You leave it on the ground for a few days maybe, get some good photos of different lighting and then sweep it up and it's done. Then all you've got is the record of it.

Alexander: How did you think about sustainability and environmental issues with this project?

Gavin: Well the bread clips aren't going into landfill for starters. It's about taking a normal, everyday, inanimate

Right: Mandala building at *Love 2014*.
Photo by Cali Pusell.
Opposite page: Finished mandala at *Love 2014*.
Photo by Ella Pusell.

little object and just not putting it into landfill but turning it into art. You take a little bread clip and times it by a thousand or ten thousand and make it into something beautiful. The only other thing I've ever really seen with bread clips is people using them as guitar picks. And I've heard of them being melted down and the plastic used for prosthetic limbs. You used to have to send them to Africa to get them recycled because it is a particular type of plastic but now there is a place in Adelaide that does it. I'm going to donate mine soon. I have about 25,000 to get rid of.

Alexander: How did you get your hands on so many bread clips?

Gavin: I just got friends collecting for me and then friends of friends collecting for me and then I find out that schools are collecting for me and I didn't even speak to that school, it was someone else who got it happening for me. There was a bank in Bowral that was collecting for me. I had no idea how that happened until a friend told me it was them that organised it. It just went a bit silly. Everyone liked the idea because it was different. A lot of people, I found out, were collecting them. They had a little jar in their kitchen because they didn't want to throw them away. They were already collecting, they just didn't have a purpose.

Alexander: What was your vision for the bread clip mandalas at the two love festivals?

Gavin: I was working with Angie on them and the vision was to just create a space. There were all these little

workshops going on. Structured times and specific sorts of things, like we're going to talk about this or we're going to have a little lecture or a dance workshop. I just wanted to create an ongoing thing in a corner somewhere where people could come and go as they pleased. Sit down, help out a little bit. Sit down and help out a lot. Whatever they wanted, just a little quiet space.

Alexander: What was it like to work at the festivals?

Gavin: They were different. At the first one I think there was Pam and me and Angie and a few others, the consistent people. Other people would come and sit down and chat to us and really not help at all, which was fine. I don't really work well in lecture environments or even circle environments where everyone sits down and tells a story. I don't like that sort of stuff but I wanted to be at love fest and so it was nice to be able to contribute in a way that worked for me.

The other love fest up at the Girl Guides camp turned into a bit of a play group with me and about eight children. I tried to focus on my piece but also let them help out or make their own thing, which turned out to be fun. I thought it was going to be a little bit more difficult than it was, but the kids were great. They were really frustrating and all over the place but a lot of fun. I didn't mind it at all. Some of the kids were very focused. Some of the kids had just had too much sugar it seemed, or maybe that was just how they were. It was lots of fun working with the kids.

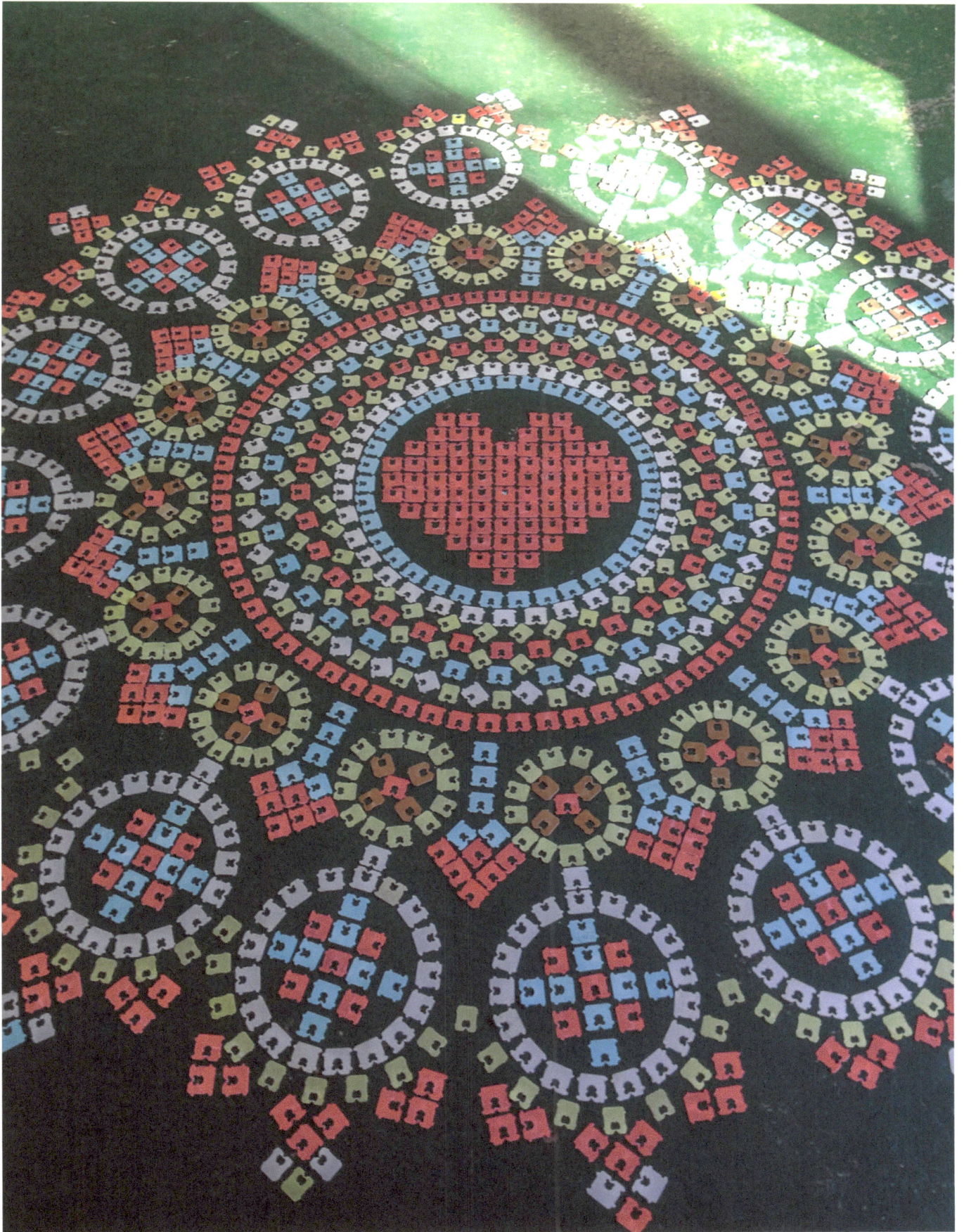

A Short Reflection on the Nature of Love Transformed at the Time of a Death or Dying

Jackie Bailey

Tender workshop at *Love 2017*.
Photo by Nina Kourea.

When someone dies, the people who are left behind can feel all sorts of emotions, some of which may seem wildly inappropriate. A few days after my sister died, I experienced a sense of euphoria which did not even feel like it belonged to me – or perhaps I did not want to admit that it did. Deathwalker and pioneer of the community death movement, Zenith Virago, explains that the feelings which come to us after someone dies – sorrow, grief, pain, anger, relief, joy, even euphoria – are all acceptable because they are all merely the faces of love transformed.

Sometimes we don't know what to do with our love when a person is dying. We might semi-consciously try to use our love to keep them from leaving us. We throw it around the dying person like a lasso, wordlessly telling them that we cannot live without them, that their dying is a selfish, irresponsible, callous act. When we touch them with this sort of love pumping through our veins, the only reason they remain limp at our touch is because they are too weak to recoil, or silently too ashamed at what we tell them they are 'doing' to us. Sometimes the best thing you can do for the dying person is leave the room. Take your love away, if you are using it as a reproach.

But love at the time of someone's death does not have to be a weapon. At a time of death, you can literally rise above yourself – you can briefly loosen your own ties to your ego, calling on your noble ancestors to help you be present to the loved one's feelings about what is happening to them.

Death is unavoidable, but that does not stop people from trying to avoid it right to the end. This can be tricky because that might be exactly what you want too. But this is your moment to see clearly what your loved one needs: help to die.

Soul midwives recommend that you touch the person: not as a way of holding them to life, but to calm them as you might a frightened horse; to soothe them with the basics of our shared being: flesh to flesh, cell to cell, wound to wound, heart to heart. You are asked by this sacred transition to calm yourself and be with the person.

If you are with the dying person, then you step into the role of companion, however brief your visit. It is not your job to pretend it is not happening, to be jocular or distracting. It is your job as a fellow mortal to see that death is coming, and to hold the dying person's hand for the time you are with them, both metaphorically and literally, and tell them with your entire being that all will be well. Not in a saccharine way, but because love at the time of death is an expression of hope.

Now is not the time to talk or think whilst in the room of the dying person, about the meaninglessness of existence or the possibility of nothingness after death. Now is the time to surrender to the mystery of not knowing. Now is the time to shrink your worldview to what is directly in front of you: that death is a path to be journeyed upon like any other.

Bring your love to the dying person as a series of small, practical gifts: a soft blanket for their feet. Dying people always feel the cold. Perhaps a mellow scented oil to soothe their senses; or some gentle music or sounds from the outside world.

Bring your love as actions. Massage the dying person's feet or hands, do their nails, brush their hair, stroke their skin.

Give your love in the things you do not do. If any of these actions or gifts seem to distress the dying person, then stop or take them away, without another word.

When someone is dying in hospital, we often call the nurses or doctors when their breathing becomes unsettled, or when their skin starts to go purple – in other words, when the person who is dying, exhibits the physical manifestations of dying. This is because we are still mentally in the mode of trying to make the dying person better. Try to catch yourself before you do this. Ask yourself what is needed to make the experience of dying more comfortable, rather than what you would normally do to try to 'help'. You are no longer required to help the person stay alive. Now your love can best take the form of small but genuine comforts. The best thing you can do is be yourself, a fellow traveller, equal with the dying person in your uncertainty and your mortality.

Love has many faces at the time of death, and the main thing you can do for the person who is dying is to turn all of these faces towards the dimming and the coming of the light.

Drawing by Siobhan Christian.

Tender Love
Jodi Phillis

Drawing by Jodi Phillis.

I cannot actually remember the first time I met Jenny Briscoe-Hough. It must have been about six or seven years ago, certainly before my mother died. I guess we met at some kind of Illawarra cultural event, an art exhibition or a musical performance. Perhaps I just heard her name through people in the community. I had heard of Tender Funerals. I loved the idea of the work they did. I remember hearing about their holistic, not for profit approach to assisting grieving families. I was impressed when I heard about their attention to detail and the tender care they gave when creating and customizing the perfect funeral service for the deceased. I did not know I would be needing their services so soon.

When we met, I knew straight away that Jenny was someone you could trust, someone you could confide in. I could tell that Jenny would speak the truth, even if it was painful. I really like that in people. I try to be like that, although I feel that I still have a bit of the people pleaser in me. I am trying to rid myself of that unwanted trait. It isn't healthy. It wastes time.

I contacted Jenny three weeks before my beautiful mother Juni died. She had been diagnosed with pancreatic cancer 11 months earlier and we all knew that she was at the end of her life. We didn't know what to do. We had never had to deal with death, certainly not the death of the most important person in our lives. Juni was a young 71-year-old. She and her husband Paul had a European holiday to look forward to in October. Juni's impending death was unimaginable and yet, it was staring us straight in the face.

I grew up with the feeling that our family was eternally youthful and healthy. It is amazing how quickly things can change. The first sign of cancer in our family was when my mother's older sister Arlene was diagnosed with pancreatic cancer, eight years prior. Arlene died within six months. We thought this was a freak event. No one would have guessed that another sister would be struck down by the same thing, not in a million years. Although I do remember hearing my mother whisper to me once that ever since Arlene died, she was frightened that the same thing might happen to her. I didn't know she carried that fear. As I get older, I have come to understand that kind of fear.

Juni was not ready to die. She loved life. She loved people. She felt she could fight and win, right up until around a month before she died. I can't quite remember what helped her to shift into that peaceful, fearless place, but it was a huge relief when it happened. Juni had lived a spiritual life, meditating and practicing kindness and empathy. When she finally surrendered to her fate, her anxieties started to drift away and we were left with a simple, radiant soul who said few words. Words full of love.

So while Juni grew in presence and acceptance, her husband Paul, my sister and I started to fall apart. How were we going to deal with this? That is when I called Jenny. Jenny's advice was to treat Juni's death like a birth. Helping someone to die requires the same kind of intense presence. 'Be there with her', she said. 'Drop everything and be by her side'.

We took her advice and while it wasn't easy to watch someone you love so much wither away to skin and bone, I am so glad that we were there with her. We spent about four days in the palliative care ward at Port Kembla until the moment she died. It was a still, sunny winter's day but the moment she died a big gust of wind howled outside the window. I guessed it was her soul taking flight. It was a super full moon that night.

Jenny and the Tender team helped us to become comfortable with the process of organizing the casket and the funeral. We chose a plain pine casket for Juni so that everyone at the funeral could draw a picture or write words of love on it. This simple ritual was beautiful and perfect for our family. Jenny was the celebrant.

At times when I felt like the grief was going to kill me, Jenny would offer wise advice, or some comforting words to let me know that whatever it was I was feeling was totally ok. In fact, she still does. Jenny doesn't know this but I see her as a kind of mentor. I'm sure many of us do.

I didn't set out to write a personal story of grief. I meant to write a few words about the love that one strong woman has given to an entire community. I guess in a round-about way, it's the clearest illustration I can draw. For at a time when my family and I were lost, adrift and suffering greatly, one woman who we really didn't know that well stepped up and held our hands.

Along with my dear soul sister Malika Reese and our lovely new friend, artist Michele Elliot, I can now call myself part of the Tender team as an artist in residence, hand-picked by Jenny. I feel blessed and so very lucky. As artists in residence we assist wherever we can using our unique skills. Michele is a visual artist with exquisite sensitivity and fine skills in the art of making, using textiles in particular. One of Michele's first experiences as a Tender artist was to sit with Dani, a 10-year-old girl who had just lost her father. Dani wanted to make a special little stitched cloth to place over her father's eyes. This transaction between the artist and the bereaved is incredibly healing. I know

Dani will treasure her time with Michele for the rest of her life.

Malika and I are the musical artists in residence. We meet with the families to decide which significant songs to sing during the funeral services. We can sing in the chapel, by the graveside or anywhere that suits the families. We can't wait for a family to request something completely un-orthodox, like having their loved one in a casket in the same room as friends and family, gathered for a banquet with live music and great food! Something Jenny often says is, 'anything is possible!'

Malika and I also run the Tender community choir, meeting every second Thursday at the Tender Funeral home. All are welcome to join. Singing with the choir is incredibly uplifting. We share our stories of grief and cherish the connection as our voices blend. Malika has also become a fine celebrant and has received expert guidance from Jenny to develop her skills.

It isn't only the community who benefit from the Tender Artists In Residence program. Artists themselves appreciate being paid for their work and when it involves helping others it is a win-win situation. In this money-driven world, it is difficult for artists to find ways to earn a living. It is well documented that artists struggle with poverty which can lead to mental health issues. Having this extra strand of income, plus being able to give to the community is positive and helpful. Jenny knows the true value of art and has the utmost respect for the people who make it.

It was Jenny's vision to bring the arts into the realm of dealing with death. This will be a legacy that will extend beyond Jenny's own life. Tender Funerals is now a template for other funeral homes around Australia, with branches opening in Alice Springs, Canberra, Northern Tasmania, Perth and one on the mid-north coast of NSW. They are independently run, following the Tender guidelines and will be supervised by Jenny.

The Tender team is growing, with more artists and volunteers offering their services. We know that the work we do is sacred … and ordinary … and important. Love is the main credential.

It is five years now since Juni died. The worst of the grief is behind me. A transformation did take place and I will always be thankful to Jenny for the love she gave during that lonely journey.

Tender Funerals: www.tenderfunerals.org

Heart Song
Perla Aura

Perla Aura's Heart Song workshop was a popular feature of both the 2014 and 2017 love festivals. Perla's voice is a stream of love that lays a pathway to the heart. percussionist. Perla is an advanced practitioner of sacred sound and vocal training whose original sound is inspired by spirit, emotion and nature. Perla tunes into intention and love to produce powerful vocals to open up a space for you to self-heal. Inspired Sound Sculptress, Perla's heart song will hold and nurture you to a world of authentic peace and connection. Holding a space to explore the freedom and joy of singing, using breath, sound, harmonies, chants, comMusication, movement and rhythm.

The sound of love resonated through the camp as 35 singers freed their voices and opened their hearts to medicine melody, harmony and connection.

We greeted each other with melody and deep listening, Heart to heart, abiding in the bliss of harmony.

This was the sound of love.

Be still, listen, allow the voice to ride on the breath of life.

Heart Song at *Love 2014*.
Photo by Ella Pusell.

Permablitz: Love in Action

Kristy Newton
(Permablitz the Gong)

Permablitz at a local home.
Photo by Sheryl Wiffen.

Imagine that you woke up one morning, made a coffee, wandered into your backyard and were greeted by multiple no-dig veggie gardens, woodchip mulched paths, chickens happily scratching in their run, and fresh seedlings poking their faces out of straw mulch when yesterday there had only been grass. Imagine then that people you knew, along with people you had never met, had volunteered their Saturday the day before to put all this together, to weed, dig, barrow, water, and plant – all so that you could have a productive, well-designed edible garden in your home. Your sore muscles remind you that you were part of this community of workers yesterday, and even though your brain logically knows that this has all come about because you have helped make this happen for at least three other households, you can't quite believe the feeling of being cared for by this community of like-minded folk. For at least 22 households in the Illawarra, this vision has been a post-permablitz reality.

At its heart, permaculture is and always has been about community – whether that is the communities of microbes present in healthy soils and compost piles, the symbiotic relationships encouraged between animals and plants by thoughtful placement and integration of those elements in design, or a community of people making small steps back towards local economies based on sharing the yields and living in harmony with the natural environment and each other. This belief in community, and a genuine desire to create something locally to try and provide a positive solution to the problems posed by a changing climate, was the inspiration for the creation of Permablitz the Gong back in 2012.

What is a permablitz anyway?

A permablitz is a community working bee held on a day where people of all ages and skill levels come together and volunteer their time to implement a permaculture design, usually in a suburban backyard. Blitz hosts will have attended at least three blitzes themselves to become eligible for a blitz of their own, and the design for the space is created by a collective of trained permaculture designers, who also volunteer their time and energy. The hosts provide the materials, cater a shared lunch, and importantly provide some cold beverages to share at the end of the day when the work is done, usually sitting on some leftover straw bales or around a newly created firepit! The mechanics of what goes into a permablitz are relatively straightforward – a host is nominated for the blitz, the design team create a design for the space, materials are gathered, the

Permablitz Workshop at *Love 2017*.
Photo by Nina Kourea.

community comes along, and everyone works hard to put it all together. What makes permablitz really special however is the intangible stuff – the conversations held while digging a swale that end up leading to people getting together after the blitz is over, the sharing of knowledge and skills that happens organically throughout the day, the warm feeling of eating a plate of mismatched curries and bread and salads and soups together with people who were strangers only a few hours ago and feeling like a part of something bigger.

The Permablitz concept has its origins in Melbourne and was invented by Dan Palmer and Adam Grubb. Permablitz Melbourne have grown massively since their inception, and Permablitz the Gong is only one of the local permablitz groups that have popped up across the nation. The core collective and design team of Permablitz the Gong was formed in 2011 by four women, Jacqui, Sheryl, Bec and myself and we held our first blitz on International Permaculture Day in 2012. In a perfect expression of the permaculture ethics 'Care for the Earth, Care for People, and Fair Share', Permablitz Melbourne have always been generous with their knowledge and experience, and shared a lot of their

documentation with us when we were getting started. Melbourne of course is a lot bigger than Wollongong and their yards tend to be smaller and flatter than some of our mountainous blitz sites so we have tweaked our processes along the way to emerge with something that suits the unique communities of the Wollongong area.

What's love got to do with it?

Permaculture is based on a set of 12 principles and three ethics: care for the earth, care for people, and fair share. These ethics are a perfect structure to describe the way that permablitz can be seen as an act of love.

Care for Earth is a central focus of every blitz. We are literally caring for and demonstrating love towards the earth through building soil, observing the landscape and interacting with it to design a system where all the elements can work together to improve the health and productivity of the landscape. Modern large-scale commercial agriculture produces food in a way that is divorced from any connection with the overall health of the environment – soils are often depleted from monoculture cropping, leading farmers to use synthetic fertilisers to feed the plants. Chemical sprays are used to control pests and diseases, at the expense

Permablitz Workshop at *Love 2017*. Kristy Newton centre. Photo by Nina Kourea.

of biodiversity and human health. Animals are rarely integrated into plant systems, but farmed intensively for maximum meat, dairy or egg production.

Permaculture focuses instead on building and supporting a holistic ecosystem that is productive in producing food for humans but also supports biodiverse communities of soil microbes, beneficial insects and animals, and plants. It is an active attempt to heal the landscape and our relationship with it. Nurturing a tomato plant from a seedling, watering it regularly and keeping the snails away, making sure it has enough sunlight and that it's growing in good soil gives you a whole new appreciation for the taste and value of that tomato. The more we understand about the complex ecosystems in which we live, the more that appreciation is taken to the next level – beyond fundamentals like water and sunlight we begin to understand that growing something flowering in your garden can attract bees which in turn pollinate your tomatoes, zucchini or pumpkins so that you get a better crop. The scraps and ends of those zucchini can be fed to the chickens, who in turn produce manure, eat weeds and bugs, and build soil through scratching and helping to break down organic matter. Increasing our connection with the food we eat through growing it ourselves and understanding what truly goes into producing it, deepens our bond with our immediate environment and our love for this amazing natural ecosystem.

Care for People is another central feature of the blitzes, and is embodied in the way the design team and blitz volunteers show love for our community by volunteering our time and energy.

Everything is easier when you do it with a blitz-worth of people power! Blitzes can be hard work for the design team and hosts and there is a lot of behind the scenes activity that precedes the blitz day. I usually look forward to the blitzes but I'll admit that sometimes I show up on the morning of the blitz with low energy, wishing that I could go back to bed rather than lead a team of people through the blitz tasks. But by the time of the opening circle at 11am I am guaranteed to have remembered exactly why we do this – the willingness of the community to show up for each other, to lend tools, help carry heavy bales and barrow load after load of mulch always energises me and fills me with gratitude. We blitz rain, hail or shine and a few years ago we held a particularly rainy blitz where it was such a downpour that we had to set up portable marquees over the garden area to even consider working. We arrived at the site that morning feeling lucky to have made it alive driving through the rainstorm, and it seemed impossible to run a blitz that day – but people turned up in full fluoro rain gear and smashed out the blitz tasks with added determination!

The community that has formed around Permablitz the Gong is truly amazing. We created a Facebook group called 'Permablitz the Gong Community' after people

Pocket planting new vegetable seedlings is one of everyone's favourite afternoon blitz tasks. Photos by Kristy Newton.

requested a way to connect outside the semi-regular blitzes and it is actively used to share resources, get advice, or call out for volunteers to help with a task that needs a few extra hands. We've seen the spontaneous birth of 'Slackerblitz', loosely organised ad hoc working bees on previously blitzed gardens where the hosts team up and help each other with maintenance without the pressure of organising a full-blown working bee. We have even had a wedding in our little permablitz family after a couple met while on the same work team and both ended up asking the facilitator for the other person's number… and the rest is history.

Fair Share is intrinsically woven into the permablitz model as it is based on reciprocal energy and labour – you give energy to at least three blitzes and then (if you want one) it will return to you in the form of your own blitz. Most of the people who have hosted a permablitz continue to come along and contribute, even through they have already received the 'reward' of a blitz. Many more continue to come along and work well after they are eligible for a blitz without ever expecting that they will get a blitz themselves – some are renters, some live in apartments, some simply don't have the space or energy for a big garden themselves but enjoy coming along to work with like minded people. The ability to access a permablitz is available to anyone who is able to contribute this time and labour – you don't even need to have money if you're willing to be patient and source enough recycled and repurposed materials for next to nothing.

The ethic of fair share can also be seen in the form of sharing surplus produce, seedlings, and resources in the growing 'Food is Free' and 'Freecycle' communities. These networks aren't organised by the Permablitz the Gong collective but are a natural fit for people who have extra vegies, hate waste, and embrace the sharing economy…and there are a lot of those kinds of people coming along to permablitzes! In a society that privileges personal gain and individual achievement over collective or communal efforts it feels almost radical to give your time and energy to community projects like a permablitz, or to give away vegetables you've grown for free. But those who do participate know that it's worth more than any transactional relationship of time for money, and that the true rewards are to be found in participating actively in a strong community.

Love in action

After six years, 22 blitzes, and a number of permabees, slackerblitzes, tours and workshops, we know that Permablitz the Gong is love in action, a demonstration of love enacted through time, energy, sweat and soil. It is love as a verb, an action of care performed predominantly for its own intrinsic value. It is revolution, one backyard at a time.

Lantern Parade
Sharon Pusell

Lantern workshop at
Fairy Meadow school.
Photo by Sharon Pusell.

I love a good lantern parade. I love the soft, warm light of the lanterns bobbing along as they're carried in procession along a dark track. There is a warmth, gentleness and simple connection with nature. It is like a river of light. There is a particular ambiance, a real sense of wonderment, togetherness and love.

I thought that a lantern parade on the Saturday night of the 2017 love festival would be a great way for people to connect and be the perfect melding of art with nature. The collective agreed, so we set about organising a lantern parade as part of the festival. We wanted as many people as possible to take part and carry lanterns. The best way to ensure that was to hold lantern making workshops in the weeks leading up to the event. We held two, two-hour workshops at a local school. Anyone interested could attend and all materials and tuition were supplied free of charge thanks to a grant we received from Culture Bank. Culture Bank follows a grass roots crowd-funding model of raising money within the community, offering an effective and simple way to nurture and develop creativity that is free of bureaucracy and generous in spirit. Participants made many interesting and colourful lanterns at the workshops and people were encouraged to come along to the festival with their designs. I also made a few much larger lanterns, including a huge, colour changing heart to lead the parade.

After dinner on Saturday night, most of the adults and kids at the festival gathered together and when all was dark on Mt Keira, in a clearing in the forest we walked in procession with our lanterns held aloft, accompanied by a playlist of love songs. It was magical.

Tips for holding a lantern parade:
- The more lanterns the better!
- Simple forms look lovely en masse
- Make sure it's dark outside.

Making a heart lantern

What you will need:
- wire
- short lengths of bamboo approx. 5mm diameter
- secateurs
- gaffer tape
- PVA glue
- tissue paper
- scissors
- sponge

Drawing by Matt Kocher.

1. Bend the wire into a heart shape and secure with tape. Try and get the join on a side as shown. Use a tin, saucepan or other round object to help shape your heart.

2. Make two the same size.

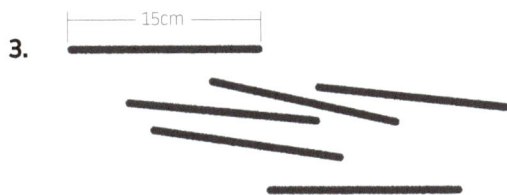

3. Using secateurs cut short pieces of wire or bamboo, to a length of around 15cm. The more rigid and straight they are the better. Make at least six, you want them to be evenly spaced around the heart.

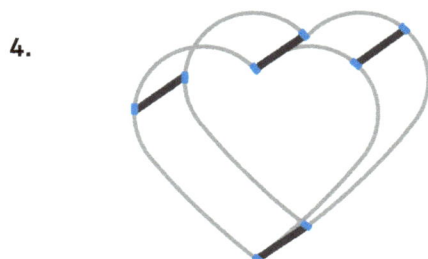

4. Place one heart on top of the other and secure together using tape with the short lengths in between. The aim is to end up with two hearts, one on top of the other 15cm apart.

5.

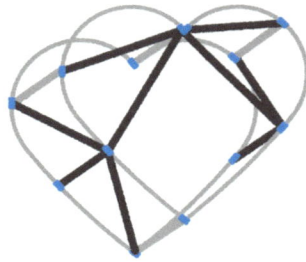

Triangles are the strongest shape. At this point you want to make your structure as strong as possible. Cut as many lengths of wire or bamboo as required to add triangle shapes to your framework. These will show up when your lantern is lit so try and make the shapes pleasing to the eye.

6.

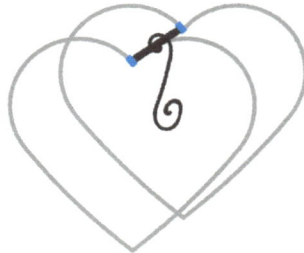

Where the top of the heart dips down you will need to attach a hook to the crossbar at the centre to hold a light source. Fashion a hook out of wire and just twist it around the crossbar. I like to use small LED lights as they are bright, safe and cheap. They can usually be found in handy key rings too. You could make another hook to hold the lantern from above or just tape a stick of bamboo to the frame and extend it out the bottom to hold.

7.

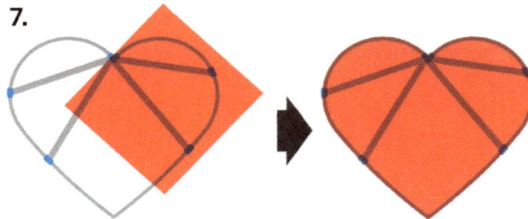

Now it's time to cover the framework with tissue paper. You could also use very thin transparent fabric. Mix up some PVA glue with water and coat the whole piece of paper with glue using a small sponge. Start from the centre and work out toward the edges, being careful not to tear the paper. Carefully lay the paper over your framework and smooth down over and around the struts. You can paper in sections, or the whole face, it's up to you. The more layers, the stronger it will be when dry. However, you don't want so many layers that light won't be able to shine through. Leave a small section at the bottom open so that you can get your light in and so you can turn it on/off.

8.

Your lantern is now finished. Leave to dry.
As the tissue paper dries it will shrink slightly and the whole structure will become stronger. You can decorate your lantern if you wish with coloured tissue paper, cut out shapes, paint or textured cloth. Just remember, anything that light won't pass through will look black when your lantern is lit, including thick paint.

Top: Lanterns on display at
Love 2017. Photo by Ella Pusell.

Above: Latern parade at *Love
2017*. Photos by Nina Kourea.

Love: A Way of Creating a More Beautiful Life

Bridget Dougherty

Bridget Dougherty at *Love 2017*.
Photo by Nina Kourea.

I became involved in the *Love: Art, Ideas, Music, Politics* festival after bumping into one of the organisers, Alexander Brown, one day in Port Kembla. I hadn't seen him for some years. When Alexander asked if I wanted to come along to the love group and perhaps participate in the festival, I had to think about it. As well as everything that was going on in my professional and personal life, I was in the final stages of doing major revisions to my PhD thesis, which explored how people negotiate intimate relationships in contemporary culture. I was very close to finishing, but I was under the pump and feeling a bit disheartened.

It was a good time to pause and reflect on why I had started writing the thesis. It had never been easy. I studied part time without a scholarship. I was a sole parent, constantly looking for work and had enough on my plate without spending every spare moment reading and writing about a subject that not a lot of people were particularly interested in, especially in academia. I nearly gave it away numerous times, especially when my ex-husband and father of my children became ill with throat cancer. I looked after him at home as best I could until he died. I supported my children's transition to high school and I continued with my research. I was frequently exhausted and the idea of quitting was a constant niggle at the back of my mind. I kept going because I believe passionately that love is the answer to what ails our society, including selfishness, greed, violence and social injustice. I kept going because I believe that without love we are mere shadows of what is possible. Meeting Alexander prompted me to reflect on how I had come to know this. Was I a hopeless idealist, an aging hippy with a fixated temperament, or was there something more to it?

My interest in love as a PhD subject, began when I was studying for an MA in Applied Ethics at the University of Wollongong in 2006. At that time, I was exploring the ethics of advertising. When I mentioned what I was doing, people would invariably say 'but isn't business ethics a misnomer?' Perhaps, but I was interested in whether it was possible to do good business in an ethical sense. Before I could understand that, I had to figure out what 'good' meant and then apply that reasoning to how business gets done. The aim was to understand how people discerned what was morally or ethically good in a society that conditions us to think that a good life involves buying lots of stuff. I was interested in whether and how individuals could live according to their own authentic values and aspirations or whether we are conditioned by culture to value only what our society tells us is good. Not a lot of people understand the extent of this conditioning. According to marketing research, the average person is exposed to around 5,000 advertisements per day, and the basic premise is that you need this or that to be happy, successful and, more and more frequently, lovable. My core question was whether people can ignore all of this and live their lives according to values they themselves choose. I had to explore the extent to which human beings are free to decide how they live.

I discovered that love had become a buzzword in advertising. This was deliberate, a strategy instigated by one of the largest advertising agencies in the world. At the time of writing my thesis, love had become the next big thing in how to sell stuff. According to Saatchi and Saatchi, the agency that invented what they called 'lovemarks', brands need to 'build emotional connections' with potential consumers, connections that people 'just can't live without'. 'Lovemarks' emerged from market research organisations pumping billions of dollars into the emerging field of neuroscience to find out how to get people to buy their stuff. These studies, which involved exposing people to images and then seeing what areas of their brain lit up, found that what motivates people is love. As a result of these findings organisations started to co-opt this primary human emotion to turn a buck. I started to notice the word love in more and more advertisements. Love had become a selling point for everything from toilet paper to hamburgers.

I found this morally questionable and contrary to what most philosophers would agree a good society is all about. We need to talk, as individuals and as a collective, about what our values are. We need robust political conversation and we need to think critically about what is going on. Advertisements that tug at the heartstrings, without people being aware that this is what is happening, may not be for the greater good and are contrary to basic democratic principles. It is also very sneaky because people do not know they are being manipulated. My main concern was that the word love, arguably one of the most important words in the English language, or in any language, was being used to sell goods, in a way that distorted our values and our beliefs about what really matters. This was the snake oil salesman in modern guise, manipulative and deceptive, and very, very clever.

My search for meaning

Prior to having children, I worked as a marketing reporter for the *Australian Financial Review*. I knew what went on behind the curtain, machinations that for the most part, people are oblivious to. I knew how

Talking About Love Isn't Easy. Drawing by Matt Kocher.

much money companies spend on finding ways to get people to notice their products, how much research and development goes into making sure their brand of toilet paper stands out from the rest. In 2019, around $560 billion dollars is being spent on persuading people to buy certain brands of toothpaste or getting them to choose one soap powder over another. The burning question for me was: when we put the word love into the mix, what happens to its meaning?

I am not alone in saying that love is one of the most powerful words in the human language. Victor Frankl in his famous book *Man's Search for Meaning*, talks about what kept him going through the three years he spent in a Nazi concentration camp. He said it was thoughts about his wife that got him through the endless days of digging ditches, with icy winds chilling him to his core. Thinking about her provided the impetus to stay alive while his body was starving and his humanity was pummelled by cruelty and ignorance. Frankl writes that one day, during a short exchange with a fellow prisoner:

A thought transfixed me: for the first time in my life I saw the truth as it is set into song by so many poets, proclaimed as the final wisdom by so many thinkers. The truth – that love is the ultimate and the highest goal to which man can aspire. Then I grasped the meaning of the greatest secret that human poetry and human thought and belief have to impart: the salvation of man is through love and in love.

This quote reminded me of Plato. Although some deride him as a proponent of totalitarianism, Plato's dialogues on love brightened my days at a time when life was very confusing. I often wonder what Plato would think of love in our contemporary times. For him, love was not the ultimate good, rather it begot the good. Plato believed that it was through love, through paying attention to what we love, that we create a beautiful life.

I think Plato was right about the importance of love in creating a society where people are free to flourish, individually and collectively, because love inspires us to pursue what really matters. It prompts us to reflect on what is real and good and true. It provides the impetus to seek happiness in the people and places that matter to us. People cannot be free if their minds are conditioned to think a certain way. If people are not free to think for themselves and engage in open conversations about how best to live, then we are indeed living in very difficult times.

Creating a beautiful life

In my PhD thesis, I argued that love is a social construct. That is, what we mean by the word 'love' is partly culturally determined. I used romantic love, a particularly Western concept to illustrate this. Romantic love is a pre-written story, based on patriarchal gender ideals and unequal power dynamics. In recent times romantic love has become infused with capitalist ideology to the extent that being lovable means having the right hair, shoes, car, job, and social media profile.

I argued that romantic love is an illusion, but that does not mean that what we feel when we experience love is not real. There is a heart beating in this body of mine, but what I make of it, is something I need to reflect on and think about. The culture we are born into influences how we think about love, but it does not determine what we value, unless we let it. As long as our choices reflect what really matters to us, as individuals and as a society, then we are free to figure out for ourselves what a beautiful or meaningful life looks like. That said, love is still regarded by many as a sentimental feeling, something that is confined to lovers and families. It is not generally regarded as culturally, politically or socially important.

There are reasons for this. Over the centuries, love in Western culture became associated with the 'feminine' side of human nature, with emotions, with sex, and with romance. It became associated primarily with women. Masculine values eschew love because it is too subjective, it is passive and supposedly clouds our reason, making us less moral and less able to discern between right and wrong. According to philosopher Martha Nussbaum, who has spent years exploring the subject, love has long been regarded in western society as the antithesis of reason. In an age where universal principles were regarded as a path to liberty, love:

…tends to be too particularistic in its focus. While liberalism seeks cool-headed fairness, love can be hot-headed and inflammatory. Love presupposes controversial conceptions of the good that liberalism (especially political liberalism) relegates to the private sphere. And liberalism means to eschew dependence on motivations as elevated as love, preferring the more prosaic motives of self-interest and respect for persons.

We now know that love is the antithesis to self-interest and central to human flourishing. It is just as important as food for a person's psychological and physical survival and thriving. Studies on Romanian orphans, for example, found that babies who grew up deprived of care, were literally brain damaged. They had a lot less grey matter, or brain cells than babies who were fostered to a caring family. The affected area, a part of the brain known as the hippocampus, allows people to regulate their emotions. Because of the damage to this area of the brain, children who are not loved when they are babies find it difficult to socialise with other children. Nathan Fox, a child development researcher at the University of Maryland, writes that children of nurturing parents have hippocampus volumes ten per cent larger than children who have experienced neglect or deprivation in early childhood.

Despite our new understandings of the importance of love, we live in a world where love has become more and more commodified. We also live in a world where we are increasingly connected to technology, but less connected to other people, especially people we can turn to when things get tough. While I was writing my thesis, online relationships, as well as social networking and dating, were becoming more and more prevalent. This has resulted in a situation where, in the words of leading cultural theorist Zygmunt Bauman, love is everywhere, but nowhere for very long. He says:

> Rather than more people rising to the high standards of love on more occasions, the standards have been lowered; as a result the set of experiences referred to by the love word has expanded enormously.

Bauman is a pessimist, but he has a point. While advertising executives are busy marrying the word love with toilet paper, intimate relationships have become increasingly fraught with violence and discord. Domestic violence, sexual abuse, terrorism, the destruction of our eco-systems, I believe, are evidence of the lack of love in our world, both in our homes, and in our hearts. In a world where people are taught selfishness as a way of life, love remains tethered to an ideology that is more about making money than it is about creating a better world. In western society we are conditioned to see love in terms of what is good for us as individuals, as a couple, and as a family, rather than what is good for all of us, as a world.

No love, no hope

As Maia Szalavitz and Bruce Perry write in their beautiful book *Born for Love*, we live in a society where empathy has become much more scarce, and this impacts directly on our capacity for freedom – our capacity to create a meaningful life through our connections with other people. Here they echo philosophers like Simone de Beauvoir, who disagreed with her lover, Jean Paul Sartre, that freedom was an individual pursuit. For her a good or beautiful life can only be realised through our connections with other people; by transcending our individual pursuits and through valuing the existence of others with whom we share our world.

> Indeed, beside every individual's claim to assert himself as subject – an ethical claim – lies the temptation to flee freedom and to make himself into a thing: it is a pernicious path because the individual, passive, alienated and lost, is prey to a foreign will, cut off from his transcendence, robbed of all worth. But it is an easy path: the anguish and stress of authentically assumed existence are thus avoided.

In other words, de Beauvoir argues that our lives have value only insofar as we see other people as having value, and importantly by demonstrating this through compassion, love and friendship. But as Szalavitz and Perry argue, in modern times empathy and kindness

have become suspect, and we are conditioned to value our own happiness, even if that comes at the expense of other people. In Western society we are taught that empathy is a sign of disease: 'even in the helping professions and psychology – where empathy would seem to be most valued – caring has come under suspicion'. These writers point to the 'co-dependency' movement as evidence of this. They argue that being concerned about others or connecting one's happiness to the happiness of other people 'in any way is actually sick'. In other words, caring is an 'unhealthy escape', or

Love 2017 merchandise.
Photo by Nina Kourea.

dysfunctional, especially when your own happiness is at stake. 'From this perspective, 'you must learn to love yourself' first and foremost. Finding yourself – not reaching out to others – is what counts'.

This is anathema, they argue, and contrary to our biological and moral good. Love matters, they say, 'fundamentally because we live our lives in relationships. Shy or outgoing, rich or poor, famous or obscure – whoever we are, without connection, we are empty'. This emptiness and the myriad ways which people seek to deny or suppress the feelings that stem from a lack of genuine connection, and which have come to be regarded as a symptom of mental illness, or evidence of co-dependency, plays out in all sorts of ways. Importantly, as I discussed above, we are encouraged to buy more stuff, and when this doesn't help, we seek out psychologists or mental health professionals to help us figure out what is wrong. As well-meaning as some of these people are, the basic tenet in our neoliberal world is that if we are not thriving, there must be something wrong with us. And if we count pharmaceutical companies as part of this ideology, treating our on-going unhappiness is worth billions and billions of dollars a year. Why tell people their depression is due to a lack of meaningful connections with other people, when you can sell them a pill instead?

Meanwhile, while organisations profit from the constant navel gazing that this ideology encourages, the real issues, the lack of opportunities for meaningful social connection in our communities, for example, become obscured by a media that is more interested in making money from advertising than it is in creating a more enlightened and politically engaged society. Issues that arise from the marginalisation of certain sorts of people, and the consequences of constantly striving for individual affluence, not to mention the social, political and environmental issues that we really need to attend to, are sidelined. Frankly, who has the time to have a proper conversation anyway?

All of this came to mind when I considered whether I should accept Alexander's invitation to participate in the love festival. Despite my exhaustion, I had come to learn that love was about connecting to other people and doing things together. It was about creating community in a world where self-interest has become the prevailing ethic. In a world where kindness and empathy have become devalued, participating in the love festival was a way of demonstrating my own values and transcending my own alienation. Despite being encouraged to see ourselves as separate and concerned only for our own happiness, for me, love is a way of potentially creating a better world, in small and significant ways. As I see it, love is the core of who we are, a way of manifesting our humanity in a world that potentially derides it.

Quantum physics tells us that each of us is connected to everyone and everything, that our very atoms are tiny specks of starlight clothed in matter, even if it doesn't feel like that sometimes. Participating in the love festival was a reminder that hope prevails, even when things get very dark. For me, it was a way back to the light.

Drawing by Siobhan Christian.

Even Though God is Love and our Hearts are Broken
Shining Rainbow

My artwork uses imagery from the natural world as a metaphor for the body and the ineffable sensations that arise within it.

Deep, deep into the forest we go – the biochemical wilderness of our hearts, our minds, our souls. Entities hover, forming and dissolving, organic and geometric, the different modalities we use to relate with ourselves and with the world.

What do we find here, in this untameable place? Personal truth – along with the sense that this truth is a fractal of some greater design, some perfect chaos.

Our truth shines like a radiant star. Or more – a sun: a solar presence that illuminates the mysterious depths of both our pain and our joy.

The relationship of the sun to the forest is the relationship of consciousness to the body and the body's deep mystery, the soul.

The healing power of consciousness to the soul is divine love.

Shining Rainbow
*Even Though God is Love
and our Hearts are Broken*
2013
Oil on canvas
340 x 210cm (triptych)

Love and Creativity

Justin Westgate

My involvement with the love collective prompted me to reflect on both the personal and political significance of love. One aspect in particular was contemplating synergies between love and creativity. Being a creative practitioner, I am interested in both functional and psychic dimensions of creative activity. On the one hand, there are general creative methods that can be employed to spark and guide the creative process, but on the other creative inspiration remains an enigmatic agency, seemingly entangled with one's inner impulses and passions. In this essay I reflect on the relationship between love and creativity, discussing significant interdependencies and suggesting that conscious employment of loving-creative attitudes remains important work for all of us in contemporary life.

There are two common associations between love and creative expression. First, love is a leading theme within creative works and, secondly – and somewhat relatedly – deep feelings of attachment and passion are viewed as a creative stimulus. Love is frequently expressed and explored through art and literature. From enduring plays such as *Lysistrata, Romeo and Juliet, Cyrano de Bergerac*, through to seminal novels such as *Pride and Prejudice, Gone with the Wind, Lady Chatterley's Lover*, and the more contemporary *The Notebook*. Such works concern themselves with the trials and tribulations of love and romantic affinities.

Likewise, poetry is a longstanding lyrical form used to convey deep feelings of affection, infatuation, or passion – a role which popular music has effectively commandeered. Innumerable ballads are impelled by love's passion: Elvis Presley's 'Can't help falling in love', Queen's 'Crazy little thing called love', Whitney Houston's 'I will always love you' and Rihanna's 'We Found Love', to name but a few. Such creative expression not only seeks to articulate powerful feelings of affection or ardor, but can be directly motivated by such sentiments. For example, John Denver's 'Annie's Song' was written as a loving ode to his wife at the time, and John Lennon's 'Dear Yoko' similarly expresses his deep love for partner Yoko Ono.

Intimate love is thus often a potent wellspring for creativity, and history is rife with examples of artists and writers inspired by relationships with some intimate muse. Pablo Picasso was notorious for his affairs with women from which he drew inspiration. Each of his creative periods is associated with a different muse. His early Rose Period works and Cubist paintings and sculptures were inspired by a somewhat tempestuous seven-year relationship with Fernande Olivier, a young woman he met near his near his studio in Montmartre.

Later, several of Picasso's most famous paintings during his War period, including *Guernica* and *The Weeping Woman*, were inspired by his then-muse Dora Maar. Other artists have similarly drawn on passionate and often volatile relationships. Édouard Manet, Auguste Rodin, Dante Gabriel Rossetti, and even Andy Warhol each found inspiration through various muses – as did prominent writers, including WB Yeats, James Joyce, F. Scott Fitzgerald, Charles Dodgson (aka Lewis Carroll) and Allen Ginsberg.

These examples serve to illustrate popular associations between love and creativity. However, within them love may often be employed through a highly romanticised frame or, within muse relationships, fuelled by passionate but problematically codependent attachments. To move beyond this, I want to consider a more nuanced understanding of love's creative potential by focusing on characteristic transcendental qualities found in both experiences of love and creative activity which productively invite us to rise above the self and the ego, and to remain open to difference, strangeness, and otherness. Expanding the ways in which we understand and experience the world leads to possibilities of extended care, responsibility and connectedness. Importantly, current conditions of planetary ecological disruption, social and political unrest and uncertainty call for such transcendental responses, which help diffuse human egoism and aid us to remain open to a world of difference, as well as alternative possibilities.

One of the challenge of discussing love is that it takes many forms. The Greeks understood this and therefore regarded love as being divided into four different categories: storge, kinship or familiarity; philia, friendship or platonic affection; eros, sexual or romantic desire; and agape, self-emptying or divine love. Drawing on this multi-dimensional framework, contemporary models similarly define love as constituted by different qualities. Psychologist Zick Rubin proposes that romantic love is made up of three attributes: attachment, caring, and intimacy. Whether we love or just like someone comes from variance in the combination of factors. Robert Sternberg's triangular theory of love also employs a qualitative triad, namely intimacy, passion, and commitment. Varied combinations of these attributes result in different types of love. For example, combining intimacy and commitment results in companionate love, while combining passion and intimacy leads to romantic love. Relationships built on two or more elements are more enduring than those based on a single component.

Jane Morris (née Jane Burden) acted as muse to pre-Raphelite painter Dante Gabriel Rossetti. Married to friend and colleague, William Morris, Jane modelled for numerous paintings, and the two had an ongoing intimate relationship.

Top left: Dante Gabriel Rossetti, *Jane Morris (The Blue Silk Dress)*, 1868. Top right: Jane Morris (née Jane Burden; 1839–1914), photographed by John Robert Parsons, 7 June 1865. Above: Dante Gabriel Rossetti, *The Day Dream*, 1880.

Having all three results in 'consummate' love: the ideal but difficult-to-achieve relationship.

Psychological analysis helps shed light on the dynamics of, and connections between, love and creativity. Psychiatrist and psychoanalyst Richard Chessick's research usefully deconstructs the multiple dimensions of love, discussing creativity as an essential component. Chessick argues that, in the first instance, love requires a *creative* leap through applied imaginative labour, where the object of one's amorous affection is in truth constructed as an idealised illusion – often shaped (and complicated) by unconscious forces such as childhood memories and relationships with parents. While not always healthy, idealisation and transference can evoke passionate feelings and energies which, as we have seen, fuel creative expression. More positively, such imaginative activity and relational play can lead an individual to expand and rewrite their personal narrative, inviting a powerful potential for change into their lives.

The activation of imagination and possibility appears to be key, and is supported by recent research which indicates that feelings of love trigger our minds to process information about the world in a 'global' or more holistic manner, stimulating creative rather than analytical thinking. Global processing involves longer-term contemplation, including wishes and desires, but in a more sustained manner given that love – as opposed to immediate sexual gratification – is driven by more caring and enduring aspirations. Love – or more specifically, a selfless, loving outlook – not only opens us up to thinking globally and through the longer term, it asks us to be open to unknown or novel possibilities, very much like a creative mindset. Thus, both love and creativity require courage to overcome the doubt and fear attached with exposing and opening ourselves to difference: new possibilities of performing or being, new values, or a reorientation of perception. Such an open, loving and creative attitude is different to the fixated impulse stereotypically perceived amongst artists. It is a state not dependant on another, but which rather calls on the individual to confront and come to terms with their own sense of self and being, and with the capacities that we each have to open ourselves to flow, to otherness, and to the possibilities found in difference.

My own recent research addresses these themes; although academic literatures by and large seek to avoid situating phenomena within a framework of love but rather employ concepts of generosity, caring, and conviviality. Such concomitant ideas are nonetheless helpful in bringing an affective dimension to the examination of worldly phenomena, opening up significant human-visceral aspects. But at the same time, this fails to attend to the important creative and imaginative qualities we have examined. At a relational level it is far easier to have sympathies for those things already close and familiar to you. Much more challenging is being receptive to and having concern for circumstances and others that are different or with which we are unfamiliar. Confronting such difference asks us not only to be open to being destabilised by the alterity of the other or strangeness, but, when combined with a creative attitude, to see them not as a threat but as a resource to help us expand our perception and behavioural possibilities of being in the world.

Being mindful of the relationship between love and creativity is beneficial for all of us – not just for artists – and in all areas of our lives. We can update outmoded tropes of love-crazed inspiration, and replace them with more productive and compelling ideas of creative nurturance. Cultivating a self-effacing loving orientation helps to foster expansive global thinking and greater self-awareness, and is the ultimate creative resource. To foster and maintain such an attitude is not easy. It requires courage and overcoming the doubts and fears of difference, the unknown and transformative change. But within such work lies the potential to not only change ourselves for the better, but at the same time to help co-create a more loving world infused with positive potential.

'Towards a Wiser Future'
workshop at *Love 2014*.
Photo by Justin Westgate.

Kindness, Happiness and a Place in the World
Alice Kocher, Ruth Kocher and Nick Southall

Children were welcome at both Love: Art, Ideas, Music, Politics festivals. During our first festival in 2014, we operated on a shared-care basis with a number of people taking responsibility for children. At the 2017 festival, the love collective gave more attention to encouraging the involvement of children with a variety of children's activities, kids' spaces, a pop-up circus playground and facilitated children's discussion about love on offer. At both festivals, children were welcome at all of the workshops. Love 2017 included events that children might especially enjoy, such as the dancing and singing workshops, the Silent Disco, the Saturday evening Lantern Parade, & musical performances. Among the Love 2017 organising collective were two young people, Alice (8 years old) and Ruth (12 years old) Kocher, who helped us to concentrate our minds on how best to facilitate the participation of children. Nick Southall spoke with Alice and Ruth about their involvement in Love: Art, Ideas, Music, Politics.

Ruth (left) and Alice (right) Kocher.

Nick: What do you remember about the first love festival (Held in Minto, 2014)?

Alice: I can't really remember much of it.

Ruth: You were really little and I doubt you can remember much of it. We were only there for a bit of it and only stayed over for one of the nights. But it was really good. I remember having a campfire, sitting around the campfire talking and singing songs. There was a really good vibe to it and I really liked that it was in the bush. In the morning we got up really early and Alison cooked us breakfast. I remember that's when our tea addiction started. We went 'hey, we like tea' and ever since we've drunk tea.

Alice: I remember sitting at a picnic table with mum and there was a boy and a girl, a brother and sister, and a few other kids and they played with us. We didn't have many kid's games. There was a big hill and we rolled down it. And one of the kids thought they saw a snake. Someone took the kids for a walk in the bush and we got to explore. I liked that it was in a bushy area.

Ruth: I know there wasn't many kids at the first one, but it did lack things for kids to do. Whereas with the second one – it was much better planned for the kids. I also feel there weren't as many workshops at the first festival. But it's a bit hard to remember everything. I would have been seven and Alice would have been three.

Nick: Do you remember helping to plan for the second love festival?

Ruth: Yes, the love meetings.

Alice: Yes, I remember going to Alexander and Mel's place tons.

Ruth: I remember we had meetings every month and sometimes twice a month.

Alice: I remember at one of the meetings we were figuring out where we were going to have the festival and I can't remember who, I think it was…

Ruth: Me.

Alice: Yeah Ruth and me.

Ruth: We thought, wouldn't it be good if we had it at the Girl Guide Camp, because I'd recently had a camp there.

Alice: It was Ruth or Mum, one of the two.

Both: I think it was Mum.

Ruth: And I remember we were in charge of planning things for the kids.

Alice: We thought having it at the Girl Guide Camp would be good, because, I can't remember, I think it was Alison that had been walking there before and she said, 'yeah it's got a really good creek and stuff' and so we decided we should definitely have it there. I said, 'yeah the Girl Guide Camp is nice' and then there was a long chat about which level, because there's two levels. We had called and neither of them was being used, so we thought which one. Ruth said there's an obstacle course at the bottom one, and at the top one there's a long walk. So, it would help me and Ruth to use the bottom one, because there'd be things for the kids to do.

Ruth: The good thing about the second one, because there was a lot more workshops and a lot more kid's activities. So, it was just more well-planned and stuff, and I think that really showed that it was better, because we noticed that all the stuff at the first festival, we were then able to make the second one even better.

Alice: Yeah. And I feel like when we were going to all the (planning) meetings there were nice gardens and these made people think about the bush. We wanted somewhere (to have the second festival) where there's grass for kids to be able to run around. And where we could pitch-up our tents.

Ruth: Yeah, the setting was much better at the Girl Guide Camp.

Alice: It was much easier, even though there was a lot of wombat poo. It was good that there was a big space for people to pitch their tents.

Ruth: We made a list of things to do for when kids were bored, with all these different activities that we were able to do at the Girl Guide Camp. There were a lot more kids at the second festival, so we needed a lot more things to do anyway. There was writing stories, letters, and drawing pictures, then sending them to refugees.

Alice: I remember we drew pictures of what you think if you had your our own festival what it would be. That was really hard for people, because they didn't know about the festivals.

Nick: So was it good to help organise the festival?

Both: Yes.

Having fun at *Love 2017*.
Photo by Ella Pusell.

Ruth: Because you got a kid's point of view. For the second festival we got to put what we wanted to do and what we thought other kids wanted to do as well. We also said our take on it. If you guys were having a discussion we would say 'oh yeah that's a good idea' or 'nah that's not'.

Alice: Every meeting we were trying and trying to make sure that they got good ideas for what to do and what kids wanted to do.

Nick: During the festival did you help out with the kid's activities?

Both: Yes.

Left: Helping out at *Love 2017*.
Photo by Ella Pusell.

Right: Circus workshop at *Love 2017*.
Photo by Nina Kourea.

Ruth: And we wore our love shirts proudly. I remember Alice and I wore our shirts and made little badges and they said 'Love festival helpers' and we were practicing, and it was a lot of fun. Mum still has photos of it.

Alice: I remember us helping out moving some stuff and doing stuff with the other kids.

Nick: What did you most enjoy doing during the festival?

Ruth: We went to a couple of workshops as well. They were really good. We did a singing one and like a yoga one, destressing and calming exercises. The singing one was in like tents, so we were outside and we would all hold hands. It was really nice and you were able to connect with a lot of other people, a lot of kids that we would have never met. A lot of adults we would have never met. And some we see a lot now. A couple of weeks ago we saw someone and we were like 'hey we met at the love festival' and they were like 'oh yeah' and Mum and Dad got talking to them. We got to make connections with people in the community, a lot more people, which I think was really good,

Alice: I like how that it was out in the bush and you got to explore, that we got to go bush-walking and workshops and it was like a lot of fun doing all the activities and the workshops.

Ruth: I loved the Silent Disco.

Alice: Yeah.

Ruth: That was really good.

Alice: I loved the lantern parade.

Ruth: That was really good as well.

Alice: Yeah. I loved how we got to make and create our own design of something.

Ruth: And all the little kids joined in and all the big kids joined in, so did all the adults and it felt like really cool cause the bush was all dark and it felt like we were in our own light inside of it.

Alice: I felt like when we were marching we were around all these other people and we'd created our own little group of people who were helping and who were our friends now.

Ruth: I remember going to the front without lanterns and like owning the parade and marching all about and feeling like ourselves and stuff. Because it felt like while we were at the festival there were no boundaries we could be ourselves…

Alice: Act like a whole different person.

Ruth: We felt really important as well. That's probably why we made a video of us practising for the Love festival. Cause we felt like we were part of something. And then when it actually happened we were like we helped organise this, we know why things are like that, we know how to do that. It felt like we were very important, we played a part, we had a role in the festival and that was really cool.

Alice: It felt like all these people asking us questions, we were super, super important.

Nick: What do you think the other kids enjoyed about it?

Alice: I think they enjoyed going to the obstacle course and having all this fun and spending time with other kids and like going to a festival and playing with lanterns and creating their own light.

Ruth: And it felt like there was a lot of space to do things, cause since we were at the Girl Guide Camp, there was room to do it felt like almost anything. So the kids probably really enjoyed that as well.

Alice: I went to the circus workshop with mum and helped to get some stuff.

Nick: Did you talk to the other kids about love?

Alice: Yes. We talked to them about 'this festival is happening because we want all this kindness to spread around the world'.

Ruth: And I felt like the other kids understood that and like we were able to tell the kids and show the kids about why we had the festival.

Alice: And that we were like connecting. That we were doing this to connect with the rest of the world.

Nick: What does love mean to you?

Alice: It means kindness, happiness, friends.

Ruth: To me it feels like you have a place in the world, you have people who care about you, who love you. But I feel like it can sometimes also mean, it can also lead to sadness, because like you might love someone and you might not be able to see them again. Or you might enjoy doing something so much that you love it. I feel like through love you're able to make a lot of connections with other people as well, especially when you're meeting new people and making new friends. You can say 'oh I love playing hockey or I love singing' and you're able to connect with other people who also have the same interests as you.

Alice: And I also feel that without love no one would ever be happy.

Ruth: You wouldn't really care.

Alice: About anybody. You would feel that you were nobody in the world, no one loved you, you're just someone who's badly treated, because there's no love.

Nick: Do you talk to other people about love?

Alice: A lot actually. I feel like we talk to people but sometimes it's very rarely that they understand what you're meaning, because there's so many different meanings of love, you can mean more than one thing when you're saying 'I love the world', you can mean tons of different things.

Ruth: Well it depends. Like with my family I feel like I do a lot. With friends it's a bit different, because I've just gone into high school and so it's like new people. But especially with friends and family, who I've known for a long time, or who I've connected to well.

Lots of kids at *Love 2017*.
Photo by Nina Kourea.

Alice: A lot of people they get a misunderstanding of what you mean. When you talk to other people about it and say 'I love you', they think that you're in love with them and you only mean that you're in love with them as a friend.

Nick: Do you think the love festivals are important?

Ruth: Yeah. Because through the workshops you were learning things like you probably wouldn't learn at school. And you're allowed to be yourself and I feel like sometimes people don't really get to be themselves because of restrictions and stuff.

Alice: I feel like the love festival's important because you get to connect and without the love festival you don't do a lot of stuff. And it's really important to show some people that you can't just be rude. That there's a lot of other people out there who love you and it's really important to be nice and helpful and that there are a lot of other talents that you have.

Nick: Anything else?

Alice: That everyone who did the cooking and stuff, they made sure that everyone who was gluten-free could eat something. They made sure that no one was left out and that everyone had something to do.

Ruth: It definitely showed there was a lot of improvement from the first love festival to the second love festival and I feel like our hard work was noticed and appreciated. Which I feel is really good because a lot of people did a lot of hard work and it turned out really well and really nicely. Can't wait for the next one.

Alice: The love festival was amazing.

Ruth: And we should do another one in the future.

Love Is a Battlefield: On the Affective Politics of Crisis

Mark Gawne

Acknowledgement of Country

This short piece was written on the lands of the Dharawal and Yuin people, and sometimes on the train passing into Eora Nation's country. These lands have never been ceded, and these are lands on which First Nations' resistance to the capitalist and colonial destruction of country and community remains powerful. The following essay speaks of violence, resistance to violence and (living) possibilities for different futures. No one has been subject to as much violence on these lands as First Nations people, and no resistance struggle has survived as long. Moreover, no future can take shape without a relation to the past, or without paying attention to the myriad living histories of struggle, resistance and healing that still carry the seeds for an emancipated future within them. Aboriginal self-determination is the first condition of any emancipatory politics in so-called Australia. Always was, always will be Aboriginal land

The present is no longer understood as a place from which to witness a coming crisis. Rather it is already felt as living amidst the storm of a deepening, runaway crisis, which feels overwhelming and immeasurable. Calculation, whether it be in the (mis)measuring of economic activity or in the rates by which we measure and realise the scale of the climate catastrophe, plays a key role in the social and subjective dynamics of political movements. But the reality of crisis is also much more than a game of numbers and measurement. Techniques of measure often have little to say about the emotional and affective cadence of crisis. And yet political movement, whether it is reactionary or emancipatory, cannot take shape without affective politics. Nothing moves without the organisation of relations and attachments between and among people, ecosystems and things. How affective politics draw on the past, arrange the present, and project a future is therefore a significant question. What follows is a reflection on the contradictory emotional politics of a world in crisis.

Dread: cycles of violence

1. The interweaving of political, economic and climatic crises underpins the new normal. The storms are cyclical and coalescing. Political crisis... Economic crisis... Ecological crisis... There is an affective, felt politics to the multiple crises of the present conjuncture. All circulate and overlap.

2. There is no clear or coherent political response to this condition taking shape that can be described as hegemonic, but rather a deepening political gulf and conflict. While multiple emancipatory movements continue to emerge, persist, disappear and reappear across the world, we are also witnessing an escalation of conservative violence and new modes of fascism.

3. The apparent universality of the climate crisis is in many respects a rearticulation of specific and uneven distributions of violence, risk, danger and deprivation that have always characterised colonial and capitalist societies. It is racialised, gendered, ordered according to territory and expressed through the cash-nexus, work and (lack of) access to social wealth.

4. The political present remains shaped by forms of control and violence that opened with the War on Terror. As Nick Southall has stated, this is a 'global war meant to have no end'. During this period there have been multiple cycles of struggle that seemed capable of generating a global re-composition of

Mark Gawne at *Love 2014*.
Photo by Ella Pusell.

political movement. However, each cycle has either given way to deep processes of decomposition, or been met with civil and global war, populism, terror and/or fascism. No wave of struggle has yet broken out of this historical parenthesis.

5. Violence is a fundamental technique in the reproduction of global capitalism, one expression of which has brought forth various modes of fascism. Violence as a technique of capitalist reproduction is nothing new. As Gary Foley notes, writing from so-called Australia, the techniques of racial governance since invasion have always organised power in modes later associated with classical fascism. Instances of authoritarian and/or fascistic thought and practice can be found from the frontier wars to contemporary carceral politics, from nationalistic and racist protectionism of the Australian labour market to the concentration camps of Australia's border regime. However, the emerging fascism of today is not the fascism of the 1930s. Endnotes once diagnosed the present as follows: 'this is a period of cataclysmic crisis for capital, yet it is one in which the old projects of a programmatic working class are nowhere to be seen'. It is worth adding that the post-programmatic period also has right-wing, populist and fascist articulations. Therefore, when assessing contemporary far-right and fascist groupings, it is better to begin with an analysis of the transformations in the forms of production, class composition, social and cultural reproduction, and the influence of all this on the actual and potential modes of fascist organisation, than it is with comparisons to the 1930s. Fascism today does not and will not look like that of the 1930s. Rather, we are witnessing various fascistic politics specific to an array of historical conditions (Modi, Bolsonaro, alt-right, etc). As Angela Mitropoulos has pointed out, one of these

modes is a post-Fordist form of fascism, which may be diffuse, dislocated, and yet remains potentially disastrous in its reach. These techniques are not coherent, but rather expressed in manifold forms: in the murderous violence of fascist nihilism which manifest in the massacres carried out by marginal individuals, through to the proximity of established fascist groupings to various governments and the central techniques of capitalist racial governance in the concentration camps of its border regimes.

6. Reactionary violence and relations are not devoid of affective politics. Rather, the formation of reactionary identities and attachments mobilises a specific type of emotional politics. Ahmed's critique of the far-right notes how 'the role of emotions, in particular of hate and love, is crucial to the delineation of the bodies of individual subjects and the body of the nation'. Southall has also pointed out how the affective turn of the 'alt-right' builds commonalities around ideas of 'purity, xenophobia, racism, nationalism, homophobia, misogyny, authoritarianism'. This is a reactionary emotional politics couched in terms of love and identity. The rightward pull and fascist tendencies make appeals to a politics of love, familiarity and shared identity for those they seek to include in the restoration of their world order. A reactionary conception of love is bound up with regimes of violence, exclusion, property, control of territory, statehood and limiting the freedoms of others.

A politics of love and commonality is therefore anything but simple: affective politics are central to political movement and social transformation, but they are also a battleground.

Joy: cycles of struggle

7. Capitalist time must be arrested. What Walter Benjamin once called the storms of progress, are now recognised as present reality by a growing multitude looking for the 'emergency brakes', to rupture and break the disastrous capitalist and colonial organisation of world-ecology, and to create an opening for a different arrangement of time: another present and future. But this will take time, effort and organisation. The urgency to act feels dissonant with the necessity to develop forms of organisation and affective politics from below that are durable within and against the multiple crises of the present.

8. The affective life of late capitalist society increasingly takes shape through sadness, grief, anger, rage and anxiety. At the same time, the movements to create a liveable world continue to emphasise the importance and centrality of love, care and resilience within the struggles for a free, common future. There is no contradiction between these respective emphases. An emancipatory practice of love is an articulation of each of these affects, from rage, grief and sadness through to joy, within a practice of healing, action, common purpose and respect of difference.

9. Struggle from below is its own form of turbulence, which moves at different rates of speed and slowness. Unrest and turbulence are produced in the movement against and beyond the general flow and order of things. To paraphrase Subcomandante Moises of the EZLN, today's rulers are dust in the wind of struggle from below.

Mark Gawne at *Love 2014*.
Photo by Ella Pusell.

10. A combination of refusal and affirmation characterises a politics of struggle adequate to the present moment. The capitalist imposition of work, its drive to exploit, extract and accumulate, animates the current crises: it is the motor force driving the train relentlessly forward. Only one response to this is appropriate: refusal. To refuse is to reach for the emergency brake. There are a million ways to do this: the blockade, the camp, the strike and so on. To take one example, today we see the strike multiplied: General strike – Women's strike – Rent strike – Debt strike – Climate strike – Social strike. The strike builds on specific forms of organisation and struggle located in a given place (workplace, neighbourhood, city, hinterland), to give conflict a common expression while disrupting the general order of things, such as the production and circulation of commodities or the sabotage of the logistical networks of capitalist society.

11. The act of refusal is only effective when it carries forward and opens space for the already existing modes of life in struggle to thrive. The strike, the camp, the blockade, the riot – each is a moment of refusal, but each is also a space for the production of new relationships, new forms of organising life and making decisions, new forms of common and communal production. From the household to the workplace and from the city to the bush it is essential to refuse, assemble and commune: to refuse the multiple modes of exploitation and oppression, to act together, and to produce and affirm caring, subversive and communistic modes of living. A communist form of love is expressed through the collective refusal and dismantling of the exploitation, oppression and disasters of capitalism, colonialism and patriarchy, while also creating things in common – that is, through relationships of care, love and solidarity with each other and with the ecosystems of which we are a part.

12. A communist practice of love aims for the proliferation of everybody's (and everything's) capacities to act towards common freedom. Sadness becomes joy through the increase of common capacities to act against and beyond that which causes sadness. Therefore, struggle itself creates joy.

For worlds in common and joy: refuse, assemble, communise.

Porridge: An Inclusive Food

Alison Jones

For thousands of years, ancient people cultivated grains from common grasses which contain nutrients essential for human development, vitality, and prevention of disease.
– Paul Pitchford, Healing with Whole Foods

Lunchtime at *Love 2014*.
Photo by Cali Pusell.

The love festivals were developed on the premise of inclusivity. Love, respect, tolerance. Through menu planning, food preparation, cooking and serving of meals, we sought to feed everyone who came to the table. Beautiful food with love.

John and I, as members of the food collective and natural early risers, took the breakfast shift, starting the preparations before dawn. Porridge was a staple. It can be eaten by (nearly) everyone and the leftovers are good for chickens or pigs. Additions of sugar, milk, yoghurt, fruit, honey, can be added by the porridge eater to their personal preferences.

From the perspective of yin/yang analysis of the thermal nature of food, grains are placed in the centre. Not too yin, not too yang, just right for breakfast, lunch and dinner. Oats can lay claim to numerous healing qualities, they have a warming nature and a slightly bitter flavour. They are excellent in soothing digestive disorders, strengthen the spleen and regulate Qi.

Porridge is not just oats, explore the possibilities of multi-grain porridge, millet, buckwheat, rye for example. Porridge made in a slow cooker is sublime. Grains are having a resurgence of interest in today's world thanks to the recognition of grains and plant-based food as a viable solution to feeding the many while minimising degradation to the planet.

We have much to learn from our Indigenous ancestors, who took what they needed with minimal disturbance, leaving enough for the next people coming through.

Both love festivals were a joy to be part of. Keys to our success were planning, collaboration and inclusiveness. The generosity of festival participants was overwhelming, whether it was helping to clean up after a meal, assisting in food preparation, or just beaming with delight as you ate our love food.

Edward Espe Brown's recipe for near-perfect porridge from Tassajara Cooking

Serves 4–6

3.5 cups of water to 1.5 cups of oats.

1–2 T of oil in saucepan.

Heat. Add oats, pinch of salt. Stir vigorously.

Add water slowly. Let the first amount to 'steam' oats.

Turn down heat.

Stir often, 15–30 min. Add more water if required.

Love Porridge. Drawing by Matt Kocher.

Above: Alison Jones serving dinner at *Love 2017*.
Photo by Cali Pusell.

Reading Love
Alexander Brown

The seed of this book was planted in 2013, when a number of people in Wollongong started a reading group. From these early discussions came the love festivals described in this book. Throughout this time, reading together has continued to provide us with inspiration as we interrogate the sources of our ideas and encounter new perspectives. In this essay, I survey the readings we engaged with between 2013 and 2018 and provide a complete bibliography. I hope that my summary of these readings will inspire you to explore the literature of love and help to contextualise the discussions found elsewhere in this book.

Our first reading as a group was *All about love: new visions*, the first in a trilogy of books on love by the black feminist writer bell hooks. hooks is a literary scholar and university lecturer who has written extensively on literature, gender, race and education. In *All about love*, hooks skillfully connects personal anecdote with political commentary and scholarly reflection as she discusses her experiences of love and loveless-ness in both her personal and professional life. When we began the reading group I, like a number of the early participants in the group, was a student and casual worker at the University of Wollongong. hooks' position as a writer who works inside the academy but struggles within and against its strictures in pursuit of deeper personal and political experiences of love helped me to think about love and liberation within my context, embracing its contradictions and seeking out opportunities to struggle for love whenever and wherever they arose.

After reading hook's book, we mostly confined ourselves to shorter essays and Michael Hardt's 'For love or money' was one of the first. In this essay, Hardt takes the common phrase 'I wouldn't do that for love or money' and observes that the saying posits an essential similarity between love and money in their power to create social bonds. In a capitalist society, money regulates social bonds through the mechanism of exchange. Love, he argues, is a power that, while often confined in purely private relationships, can be liberated so as to enable the production of a multitude of loving relationships. These ideas are part of Hardt's broader rethinking of love as a political concept in collaboration with the philosopher Antonio Negri. We turned next to their book *Commonwealth*, where they argue for the need to reclaim love for politics. In this work they draw inspiration from the power of love in poor communities, where 'solidarity, care for others, creating community, and cooperating in common projects is … an essential survival mechanism'.

Love for these two philosophers is not just a feeling, but an economic activity which facilitates survival and produces new forms of social life. They warn, however, that when love is directed only towards the same and when it is confined within the couple, the family, the race or the nation, it can produce exclusive communities in which differences are subsumed and suppressed by the act of union. For Hardt and Negri, love's great potential as a force for liberation lies in the love of the stranger: a love of difference that creates connections without requiring the sacrifice of our individuality in the way that romantic and mystical conceptions of love tend to do.

Hardt and Negri's writings on love were a major inspiration for one of our readers, Nick Southall, who provided us with a series of stimulating essays. In 'Capital and Love', Nick explores the way capitalist culture produces lovelessness and then sells love back to us as a commodity. In 'Love and revolution', he looks at love as a form of power which emerges within social struggles and at the ways in which love can enhance our lives and make our struggles joyful. Finally, in his essay 'After the 'Summer of Love': 1968 and beyond', Nick argues that the spirit of political love that developed during the late 1960s appeared not only in the stereotypical examples of 'flower power' and casual sex but 'involved a reinvention of the concept of love, from one of narrow emotional attachments to understandings and practices of love as struggles for community, cooperation, and mutual support'. Nick notes that history can serve as 'a guide to remembering the future', with the legacies of the summer of love living on in the struggles for peace and against corporate globalisation. Having looked at one historical struggle for love, we went further back still with our next piece, Russian revolutionary and feminist Alexandra Kollontai's 'Sexual relations and the class struggle', composed in 1921. In the early years of the Soviet period, Kollontai was a prominent fighter for sexual liberation and women's rights and argued against the prevailing socialist orthodoxy that the struggle for gender equality had to be deferred until after the establishment of a socialist society. She criticises bourgeois sexual morality, which she saw as being based on two principles: 'the idea of 'possessing' the married partner'; and 'the belief that the two sexes are unequal'. She saw the potential in the revolution of which she was a part to support the formation of 'relationships based on the unfamiliar ideas of complete freedom, equality and genuine friendship' (Kollontai 1977).

We turned next to Fran Peavey's 1986 book *Heart politics*. Peavey describes her political awakening as a journey towards connectedness with others. She began this journey in the heyday of the civil rights movement and later became embroiled in the campaign against the Vietnam War. These experiences taught Peavey to value connectedness above all else. It

Alexander Brown at *Love 2014*.
Photo by Ella Pusell.

is this idea which forms the basis of her 'heart politics'. In the battle to save a residential hotel that was home to older migrant workers from development, Peavey noted that the campaign's strength depended upon the community the tenants had established for themselves. Nevertheless, heart politics 'does not make politics clear and simple' and in this campaign she had to grapple with deep internal conflicts within the residents' community and between different groups of supporters. Later, in a community project to build and maintain a public park for homeless people, Peavey learned that heart politics also forces us to share in the pain of others. 'The pain of working at Sixth Street Park', she explains, 'was the pain of connection, the pain of loving people. Before I worked there, I had felt a different kind of pain—the pain of separateness, of being cut off from a whole group of my neighbours'. When the park was condemned and its homeless users were evicted she encountered a third

Fire talk at *Love 2014*.
Photo by Ella Pusell.

type of pain, 'the pain of broken connection'. Peavey's heartfelt politics enable a deeper understanding of the complexities of love. She reminds us that love does not necessarily make our relationships easier and that forging deep connections also forces us to grapple with our shared pain.

After the first *Love: Art, Ideas, Music, Politics* festival in 2014, we started another round of reading with Sara Motta's article on the women in Venezuela who have self-organised and democratised the provision of care and thereby shifted the space of politics 'firmly to the place of the community and the objectives of politics to a democratisation of social reproduction'. Motta wrote the article in response to the challenge she faced when attempting to present a paper at a Marxist conference in Sydney, which she was unable to attend due to a lack of childcare. Her work highlights the need for attending to care at a practical level in radical organising. Care and care work were important themes in much of our subsequent reading. In Elizabeth Kincade's review of feminist psychologist Carol Gilligan's book *Joining the Resistance*, she explains that 'the opposite of patriarchy is democracy. The

opposite of power over and hierarchical structures is power with and egalitarianism' and calls for a 'feminist ethic of care to re-connect both men and women with their inner selves, with each other and with a sense of responsibility and commitment to humanity'. Many participants in the reading group are engaged in care work either at home or in the workplace and these readings prompted conversations about how a politics of love and a feminist ethic could inform our work as carers. They also influenced our approach to organising the love festivals, which we conceived of as spaces of mutual care which could only function if everybody contributed to the work of caring for one another.

Our next few readings ranged widely over the literature of love. Heiji J. Nast looks at the explosion of pet culture in post-industrial capitalist societies, in particular the United States, and suggests that the love people are lavishing on pets through investing in the latest pet equipment and the fetishisation of pet love in celebrity culture conceals a failure to love and care for people in poverty. She characterises the particular form of love wealthy people in hyper-commodified societies lavish on their pets as 'dominance-affection-love' and notes that relationships 'with pet-animals are today linked to post-industrial forms of hypercommodification and alienations'. Our next 'reading' was Spike Jonez's film *Her*, which explores another side of the commodification and alienation of love in contemporary society. Through an examination of the relationship between a writer and an artificial intelligence, the film takes seriously our growing relationships with digital others. While exploring the vulnerabilities and alienation that drive the film's male lead to develop an intimate relationship with a computer program, it also allows the complexities of this mutually fulfilling relationship to unfold on screen without judgement.

Religion is one of the few domains in modern society where love is discussed seriously and so readings from religious traditions also formed part of our selection. Barry Magid draws on Buddhist ideas in his discussion of relationships, explaining that rather than trying to 'gain' something from our relationships by seeking to possess a partner or the love we create with them, we should see relationships as providing us with the opportunity to be open to growth and change through our encounter with others. 'Buddhism', he explains, 'asserts that as we are all connected and interdependent, none of us can do it all on our own'. Joshua Inwood rehabilitates Martin Luther King's broader political vision, centred on a notion of the 'Beloved Community' which originates in black liberation theology. King is best remembered for his role in the civil rights movement, but Inwood reminds us of his critique of economic inequality and militarism. Notions of community are ever-present in today's world, but Inwood points out that contemporary ideas of community tend to romanticise it, seeing it as a panacea for the ills of an alienated and atomised neoliberal society when they do not dismiss it entirely. African American communities, on the other hand, developed around a shared understanding of 'communitarian unselfishness' upon which King drew when posing the idea of the beloved community as 'a sense of community were all lives are interconnected and respected'. This vision of a community actively forged in struggle seems critical to the politics of love we have been trying to develop through our own practice.

When we came together again in 2016 to plan a second love festival, our organizing collective decided to reconvene the reading group to guide us in our planning for the event. We began with two pieces from *ROAR Magazine*. In the first, Sylvia Federici and Marina Sitrin (2016) focus on the concept of social

Alexander fire talk.
Photo by Ella Pusell.

reproduction. They discuss the growing importance of care in communities of struggle and the contradiction between the imperative to reproduce ourselves as labour power for capital and the need to reproduce social relations autonomously from capital. Calling for a struggle that is 'between the wage and the common', Federici suggests that struggles to improve our material well-being must be accompanied by efforts to expand the sphere of autonomous self-reproduction. In the second, Carlos Declos looks at an organization of migrant street vendors in Barcelona who are trying to do just that. These informal workers practice mutual aid by providing one another with practical support, sustenance and accommodation. They formed the Popular Union of Street Vendors to resist the criminalisation of their livelihoods. These readings were chosen in part thanks to a series of conversations in the organizing collective about the role of money in creative practice and the way precarious livelihoods and generalized scarcity force creative workers to charge for their work in order to support themselves and thereby creates barriers to participation for the growing number of people struggling to make ends meet. These readings informed our efforts at the love festivals to keep the cost of participation extremely low, admitting those without means for free. Organisers and workshop presenters alike contributed financially to the festivals and nobody has received remuneration for their work, thereby removing the festival from the logic of monetary exchange.

Of course, the voluntary work that our reading group members have contributed to the love festivals and to many other projects have at times resulted in forms of activist burnout. As we struggle to care for others and share in one another's pain, we have to confront the question of care for the self. Laurie Penny's (2016) essay 'Life-hacks of the poor and aimless' addresses this topic. Penny critically interrogates the notion of self-care, finding much to agree with in radical critiques of the wellness industry, with their presumption that self-care is solely an individual responsibility. Nevertheless, she defends practices of self-care in the face of nihilism and self-destruction, which are so often present in activist communities. She notes that queer communities can provide a model for collective self-care, as many of these communities have 'long taken the attitude that caring for oneself and one's friends in a world of prejudice is not an optional part of the struggle – in many ways, it is the struggle'. Vikki Reynolds, an activist and therapist based in Canada further interrogates the boundary between care of the self and care for others through her claim that activist and care worker burnout is a product of injustice. She opposes drawing strict boundaries around the work of caring professionals and advocates instead for the incorporation of social justice activism into therapeutic work. 'Our collective sustainability', Reynolds argues, 'can be fostered by giving ourselves room to experience and practice our work on the basis of revolutionary love'. In conversation with Sekneh Hammoud-Beckett, she advocates the formation of solidarity teams who can support one another even across differences and hierarchies, sharing 'struggles, heartbreak and joy in our work'.

One of the important struggles for love in Australia during the period in which we were reading and organising the love festivals was the marriage equality campaign, which sought to extend marriage rights to all couples, regardless of their sexual orientation.

Marriage equality was finally achived in 2017, the year after we read Grossi's survey of the debate over the legalisation of same-sex marriage in Australia. For conservative opponents of same-sex marriage, the institution is founded on the principal of procreation. However, Grossi discusses the way marriage came to be connected with diverse notions of love in modern societies. While romantic love as an ideal has its origins in discourses of courtly love, it is increasingly associated with ideas of freedom and equality. Nevertheless, feminist and queer writers in particular have pointed out the ways in which love can serve as a cover for patriarchal practices and heteronormative ideas which devalue the diversity of human relationships. While acknowledging these criticism, Grossi points to the enduring popularity of love, arguing that it is possible to build on democratic understandings of it. Doing so requires us to resist the heteronormative association between love and complementarity. We also read Luke Goode's piece on the ethics of hacktivism: the political practice of movements such as Anonymous who have taken action mainly online in response to issues of privacy, internet freedom and government corruption. The discussion of love here is focused on ethics and the tensions that can exist within this online community between nihilism and idealism; utopia and dystopia; individualism and collectivism; and positive and negative liberties.

In 2017 we debriefed from our second love festival while reading an editorial from the Canadian radical journal *Upping the Anti*. Like Penny, the authors focus on self-care and suggest that we also need to develop collective forms of care. They ask how can we can approach activism and community building without reproducing the logics of capitalist work that lead to burnout in the first place. This was a particularly personal article for me as I felt quite burnt out after the second love festival. The ability to come together and share these feelings with the close friends and comrades who helped make the festival happen enabled me to process these feelings and heal, demonstrating how reading groups can provide a space for collective care and support. Sylvia Federici's interview on 'joyful militancy', which we read as we met to start the discussions for this book project, addresses similar themes. She notes the prevalence of 'sad politics' on the left, and the way this sad politics is rooted in a purely oppositional activist orientation and a tendency to martyrdom. She contrasts this with 'joyful politics', which she explains, 'is politics that change your life for the better already in the present'.

My involvement in revolutionary politics has always been first and foremost a response to experiences of sadness and alienation in my own life and in that of the people I care about most. Over time, I came to understand the root cause of so much of this pain lay with the system bell hooks so aptly defines as imperialist white supremacist capitalist patriarchy. Reading love with the many different people who have taken part in the group over the years facilitated a collective reflection on long personal and institutional histories of struggle alongside new and creative engagements with contemporary movements. Through reading love, I built more loving relationships with my fellow readers. By reflecting on the politics of joy and sadness with others in a loving way, I have learned to accept that struggle can and does encompass moments of both.

Love reading list

Her, 2013, motion picture, Warner Bros. Pictures.

Delclos, C. 2016, 'The street syndicate: re-organizing informal work', *Roar Magazine*, no 2, pp. 55–67, https://roarmag.org/magazine/the-street-syndicate-re-organizing-informal-work/

Federici, S. & M. Sitrin, 2016, 'Social reproduction: between the wage and the commons', *Roar Magazine*, no 2, pp. 34–43, https://roarmag.org/magazine/social-reproduction-between-the-wage-and-the-commons/

Federici, S. 2018, 'Feeling powers growing: an interview with Sylvia Federici', *Joyful Militancy: thriving resistance in toxic times* blog, 3 June, https://joyfulmilitancy.com/2018/06/03/feeling-powers-growing-an-interview-with-silvia-federici/

Goode, L. 2015, 'Anonymous and the political ethos of hacktivism', *Popular Communications*, vol. 13, pp. 74–86.

Grossi, R. 2012, 'The meaning of love in the debate for legal recognition of same-sex marriage in Australia', *International Journal of Law in Context*, vol. 8, no 4, pp. 487–505.

Hardt, M. 2011, 'For love or money', *Cultural Anthropology*, vol. 26, no 4, pp. 676–682.

Hardt, M. & A. Negri, 2009, 'Of love possessed', in *Commonwealth*, The Belknap Press, 2009, pp. 179–188.

hooks, b. 2001, *All about love: new visions*, HarperCollins Publishers.

Inwood, J.F.J. 2009, 'Searching for the promised land: examining Dr Martin Luther King's concept of the beloved community', *Antipode*, vol. 41, no 3, pp. 487–508.

Kincade, E.A. 2013, 'Resistance refined, patriarchy defined: Carol Gilligan reflects on her journey from difference to resistance (A review of *Joining the Resistance* by Carol Gilligan, Polity Press, 2011)', *Sex Roles*, 68, pp. 275–278.

Kollontai, A. 1977, 'Sexual relations and class struggle', in *Alexandra Kollontai: selected writings*, Allison & Busby, https://www.marxists.org/archive/kollonta/1921/sex-class-struggle.htm

Magid, B. 2008, 'No gain: relationships won't solve our problems, but they can make us grow', *tricyle*, https://tricycle.org/magazine/no-gain/

Motta, S. 2013, 'We are volcanoes: transgressing the silence of motherhood', *venezuelanalysis.com*, https://venezuelanalysis.com/analysis/10105.

Nast, H.J. 2006, 'Loving ... whatever: alienation, neoliberalism and pet-love in the twenty-first century', *ACME: An International E-Journal for Critical Geographies*, vol. 5, no 2, pp. 300–327.

Peavey, F. 1986, *Heart politics*, Black Rose Books, Montreal.

Penny, L. 2016, 'Life-hacks of the poor and aimless: on negotiating the false idols of neoliberal self-care', *The Baffler*, 8 July, https://thebaffler.com/latest/laurie-penny-self-care

Reynolds, V. 2011, 'Resisting burnout with justice-doing', *International Journal of Narrative Therapy and Community Work*, no 4, pp. 27–45.

Reynolds, V. and S. Hammoud-Beckett, 2012, 'Bridging the worlds of therapy and activism: intersections, tensions and affinities', *International Journal of Narrative Therapy and Community Work*, no 4, pp. 57–61.

Southall, N. 2010a, 'Love and revolution', *Links: international journal of socialist renewal*, https://revoltsnow.wordpress.com/2010/11/17/love-and-revolution/

Southall, N. 2010b, 'After the 'Summer of love': 1968 and beyond', *Revolts now: a multitude of possibilities*, https://revoltsnow.wordpress.com/2010/08/24/after-the-summer-of-love-1968-and-beyond/

Southall, N. 2019, 'Capital and love', *Revolts now: a multitude of possibilities*, https://revoltsnow.wordpress.com/2019/06/01/capital-and-love/

Upping the Anti, 2016, 'Who cares? the politics of care in radical organizing', *Upping the Anti*, no 18, October 11, https://uppingtheanti.org/journal/article/18-editorial/

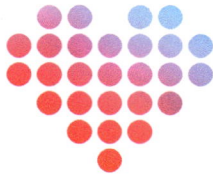

Lightning Source UK Ltd.
Milton Keynes UK
UKHW050255080620
364547UK00005B/69

9 780648 825807